SURPRISING FACTS FOR BRAINY PEOPLE

History, Society, Pop Culture & More: 1000+ Utterly Mind-Blowing Facts and Unbelievable Information That Will Leave you Speechless (and Arguably Smarter)

- Albert Junius -

Table of Contents

DO YOU THINK YOU KNOW EVERYTHING?

THINK AGAIN!

From unexplored creatures to eerie places, this book will take you on a journey through the most incredible and mind-blowing facts that are guaranteed to astound.

Dive into a world of astonishing information and explore topics like science, mythology, history and more!

Whether you are an avid learner or simply looking for some fun facts to impress your friends, this book is the perfect blend of knowledge and entertainment!

Get ready to be amazed by the extraordinary information inside.

Are you ready to get smarter, wiser and absolutely dominate every trivia game?

Let's go!

The journey begins now!

Roman Empire

- The Roman Empire was the largest and most powerful in history, with its boundaries extending from Northern England to North Africa and from Mediterranean Sea to the Middle East. It lasted for more than 500 years (27 BC - 476 AD) and at its height, it covered over 2 million square kilometers of land.

- The Roman Empire was an autocratic government, with an emperor at its head who had absolute authority. One of the most famous and powerful emperors was Julius Caesar (100–44 BC).

- The Roman Empire had a complex system of social classes that divided people into patricians (the elite upper class) and plebeians (the common people).

- The Roman Empire was a major contributor to the development of law. It introduced laws that were followed throughout its provinces, such as the Twelve Tables and Justinian Code.

- The Latin language, which is the basis for many modern languages, was derived from the ancient Roman language called Vulgar Latin.

- The Roman Empire was heavily influenced by the Greeks, in terms of culture and technology. Many innovations like running water, public baths, sewage systems, temples etc., were adopted from the Greeks and spread throughout their provinces.

- By 55 BC, the Romans had conquered an empire that stretched across Europe and the Mediterranean.

- Roman engineering was so advanced that they were able to build over 50,000 miles of roads throughout their empire, connecting provinces and allowing for the spread of goods and services.

- The Romans also built aqueducts that allowed them to bring water from rivers or streams into cities or towns.

- Rome was the center of Christianity during this period, with St. Peter's Basilica being built by Emperor Constantine in 326 AD and later becoming the seat of the Catholic Church.

- The Romans were known for their sophisticated art and architecture, including works such as the Colosseum and Pantheon.

- The Roman Empire was responsible for the spread of Christianity in Europe and beyond, with Emperor Constantine making it the official religion of Rome in 313 AD.

- Gladiatorial combat and chariot racing were popular forms of entertainment during the Roman period, and were held in large amphitheaters like the Colosseum.

- Roman mythology was very influential and is still seen in many aspects of modern culture, such as the names of gods and goddesses being used for months of the year, days of the week and planets in our solar system.

- Rome itself was known for its grandeur and decadence, with many emperors building monuments and palaces to celebrate their power. There were also public festivals, like the Saturnalia, where people celebrated with food, wine and music.

Middle Ages

- Between the 11th and 13th centuries, most of Europe was organized into feudal systems with a strict hierarchy of nobility and serfs. Monarchs granted land to powerful noble families in exchange for military service and financial resources. These families in turn gave their own serfs some small plots of land from which they drew sustenance.

- In the Middle Ages, most books were written in Latin, and only a select group of educated people could read them. Thus, knowledge was concentrated in the hands of the powerful clergy and nobles who had access to education and resources.

- The Black Death is widely recognized as one of the worst pandemics in human history, killing an estimated 75 to 200 million people across Europe. The disease was spread through fleas that infected rats, which came into contact with humans and passed the bacteria on to them.

- During the Middle Ages, the Catholic Church was a powerful and influential force in European politics and culture. The two most important figures were the Pope and the Emperor, with both of them claiming temporal and spiritual power over Europe.

- The medieval period was a time of great social mobility for women in European society, as they could become queens, abbesses and even merchants. Women in the Middle Ages also held important positions in law courts, had their own property and were able to travel relatively freely.

- Jousting was a popular sport among the nobility during the Middle Ages, with knights competing in tournaments for fame and glory. The jousts involved two armoured knights riding horses at each other and attempting to unhorse their opponent using blunted lances.

- In medieval Europe, guilds were a form of organization for craftsmen and merchants to work together in the same trade. Guilds provided members with protection, educational events and regulations to ensure the safety and quality of their goods.

- During the Middle Ages, education was focused mainly on religious knowledge, such as Latin grammar and scripture study. Schools were run by churches or monasteries, and only wealthy families could afford to send their children to learn in them.

- The Hundred Years' War was a long conflict between England and France that lasted from 1337 to 1453. During the war, many battles were fought on land and at sea, with huge losses of life and property on both sides.

- The Roman Empire had left a great legacy in medieval Europe, including infrastructure, laws, language and culture. Many European countries still use Latin-based languages today and look to ancient Rome as the source of their legal system.

- In medieval Europe, castles were built as strongholds against invaders and to protect wealthy families. Castles were large, fortified structures consisting of thick walls, moats, drawbridges and lookout towers.

- During the Middle Ages, most Europeans were farmers who worked the land by hand in order to feed their families. This was an incredibly laborious task that required knowledge of crop rotation, manuring and other agricultural techniques.

- In the medieval period, diseases like plague, smallpox and leprosy were widespread throughout Europe. These illnesses killed millions of people, but there were no effective treatments available at the time to combat them.

- Medieval art was a reflection of the religious and cultural values of the time, with many pieces depicting Biblical scenes or hieratic figures. Artists made use of a wide range of materials, including wood, stone and metal.

- In medieval Europe, towns were places of commerce and refuge for those fleeing oppressive governments or violent conflicts. Towns had their own administrations, laws and systems of governance, and provided protection to their inhabitants.

- The Crusades were a series of military campaigns fought by Christian forces from Europe against the Muslim states in the Middle East and North Africa. The Crusades lasted for two centuries and led to great losses of life on both sides.

- In medieval Europe, religious pilgrimages were a popular form of devotion. Thousands of Christians would make the journey to holy sites in places like

Jerusalem, Rome and Santiago de Compostela in order to show their devotion and seek grace from God.

- The invention of the printing press during the 15th century revolutionized European culture, as it allowed for the mass production of books and other materials. This enabled knowledge to spread more quickly and widely than ever before, leading to an increase in literacy rates.

- During the Middle Ages, knights were members of a warrior class who fought alongside kings and lords in battle. Knights were expected to abide by a code of honor known as chivalry, which included loyalty, bravery and respect for women.

World War 2

- World War II was the deadliest conflict in human history, with an estimated 80 million casualties. It resulted in the deaths of approximately 50 million military personnel and civilians. While most of those casualties were from combat, about one-third were due to genocide and other war crimes committed by Nazi Germany against Jews, homosexuals, and other ethnic and religious groups.

- The Battle of Stalingrad, which lasted from August 1942 to February 1943, was one of the longest and bloodiest battles in World War II. Over 1 million soldiers died during the battle, with some estimates placing the number even higher.

- During World War II, over 12 million people were forcibly relocated to Germany by the Nazi regime. This number includes not only Jews but also ethnic Germans, Poles, and other Eastern Europeans.

- Approximately 500,000 women served in military roles during World War II. The majority of these women were nurses, while some also served as pilots, mechanics, radio operators, and other non-combat roles.

- The Japanese attack on Pearl Harbor, which took place on December 7th, 1941, was one of the most important events that led to the US joining World War II. As a result of this attack, 2,403 American citizens were killed and 1,178 were wounded.

- The atomic bombings of Hiroshima and Nagasaki, which occurred on August 6th and 9th, 1945 respectively, marked the first time that nuclear weapons were used in warfare. As a result of these bombings, between 129,000 and 226,000 people lost their lives.

- The Battle of Britain was one of the most significant battles in World War II. This battle was fought between the Royal Air Force and the German Luftwaffe for control of the skies over England from July to October 1940.

- The Battle of the Bulge, which lasted from December 16th, 1944 to January 25th, 1945, was one of the largest battles that took place during World War II. Over 1 million soldiers from the US, UK, and Germany were involved in this battle.

- The Allies declared victory in Europe on May 8th, 1945 after Germany's unconditional surrender. This day is now known as V-E Day (Victory in Europe Day).

- On August 15th, 1945, Japan announced its surrender to the Allies, marking the end of World War II. This day is now known as V-J Day (Victory over Japan Day).

- During World War II, almost every major country was involved in some way or another. In total, there were 50 countries and 17 colonial territories that fought on either side of the conflict.

- Approximately 16 million Americans served in World War II, making it one of the largest mobilizations in US history. Of those 16 million, approximately 500,000 were killed during the war and over 400,000 were wounded.

- The D-Day landings, which took place on June 6th, 1944, was the largest seaborne invasion in history. Over 156,000 Allied troops participated in this operation, which eventually led to the liberation of Europe from Nazi control.

- The Holocaust was one of the most devastating events of World War II and resulted in the deaths of approximately 6 million Jews as well as other ethnic and religious minorities. This genocide was carried out by Nazi Germany and its accomplices throughout Europe.

- The Nuremberg Trials were held from November 1945 to October 1946 in order to prosecute those responsible for war crimes committed during World War II. 24 high-ranking Nazi officials were tried at these trials, of which 12 were sentenced to death.

MYTHOLOGY

Greek Mythology

- The Greek Gods were a family, with all sorts of relationships between them. Zeus was the father of all gods and ruler of Mount Olympus. His siblings included Poseidon, the god of the seas; Hades, the god of the underworld; Hera, his wife and goddess of marriage; Demeter, goddess of harvest; Hestia, goddess of the hearth and home; and Aphrodite, the goddess of love.

- The gods had special powers that helped them shape human destiny. Each of them could also be represented by animals or objects — for example, Zeus was associated with the eagle and thunderbolts, Poseidon with horses and tridents, and Aphrodite with doves and mirrors.

- In Greek mythology, gods were not always good: they had human-like emotions and weaknesses, such as vanity and jealousy. They could be vengeful, often punishing mortals for their misdeeds

- The gods of Ancient Greece took part in many adventures and the tales of these adventures often provided entertainment to the Greek people. One of the most famous stories is that of the Trojan War, a war between Greece and its neighboring city-state Troy.

- Ancient Greeks believed in many different gods and goddesses who were each responsible for certain aspects of life, such as love, fertility, healing and death. Many of these gods and goddesses have been worshiped for thousands of years.

- Ancient Greek mythology tells stories about monsters, such as the Minotaur, a creature with the head of a bull and the body of a man; Cerberus, a giant three-headed dog that guards the entrance to Hades; Chimera, a fire-breathing creature made of a lion, goat and snake; and the Hydra, a giant serpent with multiple heads.

- Ancient Greek mythology is filled with incredible stories about heroes and their feats of strength, courage and skill. These heroes were often portrayed as larger-than-life figures who could defeat monsters or perform amazing tasks. One of the most famous heroes is Hercules, a half-god with superhuman strength.

- Ancient Greeks believed in fate, the idea that certain events were predetermined and out of their control. This belief was often used to explain why bad things happened or why people couldn't change their lives.

- Ancient Greeks also believed in omens, signs that could foretell the future or give advice on how to make difficult decisions. Many of these omens, such as a special bird call, were interpreted by respected prophets.

- In Greek mythology, the gods had many sacred sites and objects which held great power and could bring good luck if they were treated with respect. These sacred sites and objects included the Oracle of Delphi, the Golden Fleece, and the Temple of Apollo.

- Ancient Greeks believed that certain plants had magical properties and could help them in their daily lives. For example, they believed that garlic could ward off evil spirits and that olive branches could bring good luck.

- In Greek mythology, there were many mysterious creatures who lived in the underworld or on the edge of society. These creatures included satyrs, fauns, centaurs and mermaids.

- According to ancient Greek mythology, people could be transformed into animals as a punishment for their wrongdoings. This transformation was usually permanent and could be done by the gods or witches.

- Ancient Greeks believed that some animals had special powers and they often used them in spells and rituals to cure diseases, protect against evil spirits, and bring good luck. These animals included snakes, cats, frogs, and birds such as eagles and owls.

- The Ancient Greeks had a great appreciation for beauty and art. They created many statues of their gods and goddesses, as well as sculptures depicting scenes from mythology. They also wrote plays, poetry, music and stories that celebrated the glory of the gods.

Egyptian Mythology

- The Egyptian god of chaos, Apep, was a giant snake that would attack the Sun during its daily journey across the sky. Apep was usually depicted as a coiled serpent with an evil glare and sometimes wings and claws. Every night, Ra, the sun god, would battle him in an attempt to protect the sun, and Ra would eventually be victorious and restore order to the world.

- The god Seth was considered a protector of pharaohs and a champion of justice. He was usually depicted as having an animal head with curved horns, sometimes wearing a red or white crown. He was also believed to be the one responsible for killing Osiris, another important Egyptian god.

- Hathor was the goddess of love, beauty and music. She was usually depicted with a cow's head and sometimes wearing the solar disk between cow horns on her head. She was seen as a nurturing figure who could bring joy to those who needed it most.

- Bastet was the goddess of cats, protection and fertility. She was usually depicted with the head of a cat or lioness and had an important role in protecting homes from evil spirits.

- One of the most important goddesses in Egyptian mythology was Isis, who was seen as a mother figure who could bring love and comfort to those in need and protect them from harm. She was often depicted with a headdress in the form of cow horns and a solar disk, symbolizing her power over the forces of life and death.

- Anubis was the god of embalming and protector of tombs. He had a human body but an animal head, usually that of a jackal or dog. He would judge souls who were entering the afterlife and ensure their safe passage to the underworld.

- Sobek was the god of crocodiles and associated with fertility, strength, and protection from all sorts of dangers. He was usually represented as having a human body but a crocodile's head, wearing an elaborate crown made up of feathers from different birds representing his divine power over the natural world.

- Thoth was the god of knowledge and wisdom, usually represented as having a human body with an ibis head. He was also responsible for maintaining order in the universe and ensuring that justice prevailed by recording every event that occurred in the heavens and on earth.

- The goddess Ma'at was associated with truth and justice, and she served to uphold cosmic order throughout the world. She was often depicted wearing an ostrich feather headdress, symbolizing her role in keeping balance between chaos and harmony in the universe.

- Sekhmet was a lioness-headed goddess associated with healing, protection from evil forces, and vengeance against those who wronged her followers. She could also bring destruction and death when needed, as she was believed to have been the one who caused a plague in ancient Egypt.

- Taweret was the goddess of childbirth and protector of pregnant women. She was usually depicted with a hippo's body and sometimes with crocodile legs. She served to ensure safe births for mothers by protecting them from any dangers that might come their way during delivery.

- Neith was the goddess of war and hunting, and also had some healing abilities associated with her role as guardian of the dead. She could be represented in two ways: as a woman wearing red clothing, or with a bow on her shoulder and arrows in her hand, symbolizing her protection from evil forces.

- The god Horus was the son of Isis and Osiris, and he was often depicted with a falcon's head. He was associated with kingship, justice, protection from evil forces, and also had healing powers. He is usually portrayed as a protector of the sun god Ra.

- Nut was the goddess of the sky who protected her husband Geb, the god of earth. She was usually represented by a woman wearing stars on her body, symbolizing her control over celestial bodies like stars and planets in the night sky.

- Ptah was the god of craftsmen and architects who served to create buildings for gods and humans alike. He could be represented either as a human or an animal, usually with a bull's head. He was also the god of creation and artistic expression, serving to bring art and beauty into the world.

- Hapi was the god of the Nile River and associated with fertility and abundance. He was often depicted as having a large belly, symbolizing his role as a provider of sustenance for humans who depended on him for their daily lives. He could also be represented with a lion's head or sporting a beard made of papyrus plants.

Chinese Mithology

- In Chinese mythology, Fu Hsi was the first ruler of China who invented writing and led the people to a better life. He is also said to have discovered fire by rubbing two stones together and created an alphabet out of symbols he found in nature. He made sure that everyone in the kingdom had enough food, shelter and other resources they needed to live happily.

- According to Chinese mythology, Nu Wa created humans from yellow clay and gave them the knowledge they needed to survive such as how to create weapons, build houses and make clothes. She also taught humans how to use fire and showed them how to fish in order to get food.

- The gods are believed to be responsible for creating dragons which symbolize strength and power. It is believed that dragons originated in China and were used to ward off evil spirits. They are also said to have the ability to control the weather and bring rain when needed.

- Chang'e, the goddess of the Moon, is an important figure in Chinese mythology. She is believed to have descended from Heaven with her husband Hou Yi who was a powerful archer. Chang'e chose to stay on the moon for eternity so she could keep watch over him from afar.

- In Chinese mythology, Nüwa is responsible for repairing a damaged heaven which was destroyed by floods caused by two cosmic creatures known as Gong Gong and Bu Zhou. After repairing it, she made five different colored stones which represented the five elements of life and threw them into the sky, creating a rainbow.

- According to Chinese mythology, Lei Gong is responsible for thunder and lightning and is also known as "The Thunder God" or "Lord of Heaven". He is usually depicted as a muscular man with wings wielding a drum and hammer which he uses to produce loud thunderclaps when angered by humans.

- In Chinese mythology, Pangu created the universe from an infinitely large black egg shaped void containing Yin Yang, two opposite forces that represent all forms of duality in the world such as light and darkness, good and evil, male and female etc.

- According to Chinese mythology, Shennong was the legendary divine farmer and inventor of agriculture who taught mankind how to cultivate crops and use herbal medicine. He also invented a tool known as "The Ploughshare" which is still used by farmers today.

- Nezha, the third son of a high-ranking military officer, is an important figure in Chinese mythology. He is said to have been born with magical powers and could transform into different creatures such as a dragon or giant bird at will. He also possessed immense strength that allowed him to fight off monsters and evil spirits.

- In Chinese mythology, Sun Wukong is known as "The Monkey King" who was born from a stone egg on Mount Huaguo and obtained supernatural powers from Laozi, the founder of Taoism. He is one of the most popular figures in Chinese mythology and is said to possess immense strength and magical abilities.

- Guanyin was an important figure in Chinese mythology who brought enlightenment and compassion to the world. She was originally a male deity of war but eventually changed into a female bodhisattva who became known as the "Goddess of Mercy" due to her compassionate nature.

- In Chinese mythology, Nügua mixed together five colours (black, white, red, yellow and green) to create humans out of mud which she then placed on Earth using her divine power. This act resulted in all living creatures including humans and animals being created.

- In Chinese mythology, Qilin is a mythical creature that symbolizes luck and good fortune. It is usually portrayed as a dragon-like creature with the head of a dragon, the body of a horse and the scales of a fish. It has long been associated with prosperity and protection from danger and evil forces.

- According to Chinese mythology, Zhang Guolao was responsible for inventing the wheelbarrow during the Tang Dynasty which allowed people to easily transport goods over long distances. The wheelbarrow still remains an important tool used for transportation today in Asia and around the world.

- Fu Xi was said to have invented writing during the ancient Shang Dynasty in China. He is also credited with inventing the game of chess as well as fishing and trapping techniques that were used to catch fish. The Chinese writing system is said to have been developed from his original script.

- Fu Hsi, along with Nüwa, was one of the earliest rulers of ancient China and was responsible for establishing many early laws which helped maintain order in society during a time when chaos and violence were rampant. He was also revered for introducing the Eight Trigrams which are believed to represent all forms of duality such as yin and yang, good and evil etc.

PHYLOSOPHY

Greek Phylosophy

- The Greek philosopher Plato believed that the ideal city should be ruled by philosophers, who would focus on making decisions for the well-being of everyone in society. He thought that individuals living in this kind of Utopian society would live a much happier and content life than those living in other cities.

- Aristotle was an ancient Greek philosopher who was a student of Plato's and also founded the Lyceum, an educational institution in ancient Athens. He is known for writing extensively on such topics as philosophy, science, mathematics, politics and ethics

- Ancient Greek philosophy had its roots in questions about morality and human nature. The pre-Socratic philosophers focused on understanding the natural world and human behavior. They believed that a person could attain truth by examining their own thought processes, rather than relying on religious or supernatural beliefs.

- The Greek philosopher Socrates is often referred to as the founder of Western philosophy. He championed the idea that individuals should question their beliefs in order to uncover the truth, which is now known as the Socratic Method.

- The Stoic philosophy was founded by Zeno of Citium in the around 300 BCE and it holds that true happiness can only be found if one is able to accept pain, misfortune and tragedy without becoming overwhelmed or losing their inner peace. It also teaches individuals to live a life of virtue and moderation.

- The Epicurean philosophy, founded by Epicurus in the 3rd century BCE, holds that one should seek pleasure, but only to a certain degree and never at the expense of others. It teaches individuals to focus on leading a life of tranquility and freedom from fear rather than pursuing material wealth or power.

- The Cynic philosophy was founded by Antisthenes in the 4th century BCE and it holds that true happiness can only be attained through leading a life of asceticism, self-control, and simplicity. It teaches that having too many material possessions or desires will only lead to unhappiness and discontentment.

- The Sophists were a group of travelling teachers and philosophers in ancient Greece who focused on the topics of rhetoric, philosophy, and ethics. They believed that knowledge was not absolute and that individuals should be taught to argue both sides of an issue in order to convince others of their point-of-view.

- The Platonic school of thought was founded by Plato in the 4th century BCE and it holds that there is an ideal, perfect world which exists beyond our own physical realm. Individuals should strive to understand this higher reality in order to lead a more fulfilled life.

- The Peripatetic school of thought was founded by Aristotle in the 4th century BCE and it holds that the physical world is all there is. This school of thought focuses on understanding and interpreting phenomena in the natural world, rather than looking for higher truths or a metaphysical realm.

- Skepticism was a popular philosophical school of thought after the Hellenistic period which holds that it is impossible to know anything with absolute certainty and thus one should suspend judgment until all the evidence is in. It teaches individuals to remain open-minded and not take things at face value.

- Hedonism was a popular philosophical school of thought during the Hellenistic period which holds that pleasure is the only true good, and thus one should strive to maximize their own pleasure while minimizing their pain. It teaches individuals to strive for balance and moderation in their pursuit of pleasure.

- The Cynic-Stoic school of thought was a blend of the Cynic and Stoic philosophies which holds that one should seek inner peace by living a life of simplicity and self-control, while avoiding material goods or desires which can lead to unhappiness. It teaches individuals to strive for balance between physical and spiritual well-being.

- The Neo-Platonic school of thought was founded by Plotinus in the 3rd century CE and it holds that a higher, more perfect reality is beyond our own physical realm; individuals should seek to understand this transcendent realm in order to reach a greater level of spiritual understanding.

- Eclecticism is an eclectic school of thought which combines various philosophical traditions from different eras and cultures; it seeks to combine the best parts of each tradition in order to create a more comprehensive worldview. It teaches individuals to remain open-minded, learn from all sources, and create their own unique philosophy.

- Existentialism is a school of thought which holds that individuals are responsible for creating their own meaning in life by making choices and taking action. It teaches individuals to take responsibility for their own lives, strive for authenticity, and embrace freedom from societal conventions or norms.

- Humanism is a philosophical school of thought which focuses on the potential of humanity and its ability to progress through education, science, and technology. It teaches individuals to strive for self-fulfillment and autonomy, while also respecting the rights and dignity of all human beings.

Chinese Philosophy

- Chinese philosophy dates back to the 6th century BC and is based on the idea of Yin and Yang which are opposite forces that explain cosmic balance. They are represented by a circle divided into two halves, one black and one white. The Ying symbolizes feminity, darkness, moonlight while Yang stands for masculinity, lightness, sunlight.

- According to Taoism which is a school of Chinese philosophy there are two ways in life: wu-wei (action without effort) and ziran (naturalness). Wu-wei requires people to accept things as they come with no judgement or expectations; ziran encourages individuals to let go of control and allow nature to take its course - much like the idea of going with the flow.

- Confucianism is another major school of Chinese philosophy which emphasizes on having a good moral character and social relationships, such as respect for elders and obedience to authority. It values five virtues: filial piety, loyalty, righteousness, propriety and integrity which are essential in order to have a harmonious society.

- Legalism is a practical system of government that focuses on rules, laws and regulations as opposed to morality or ethics like other Chinese philosophies do. The goal was to create an efficient state where people would be obedient and follow orders without questioning it.

- Daoism also known as "The Way" suggests that human beings should strive towards living in harmony with nature. It is a religious philosophy which emphasizes on the concept of harmony between man and nature as well as self-cultivation.

- According to Chinese philosophy, human beings are part of something bigger than themselves which is called "The Way" or Taoism. This school of thought suggests that people should strive towards living in harmony with nature and accept life's ups and downs without worrying too much about it.

- In Chinese philosophy, there is a strong emphasis on personal integrity and virtue, rather than relying solely on laws and regulations for social order like Legalism does. Confucianism believes in the importance of morality and ethics when forming relationships with others, while Daoism suggests that people should strive to cultivate their inner self in order to achieve balance and peace.

- Another major concept in Chinese philosophy is the idea of Yin and Yang, which symbolizes two opposite forces that influence one another while still managing to remain in harmony with each other. This duality means that everything has its opposite but it must be balanced for life to work properly.

- In Chinese philosophy, there is great value placed on the idea of "wu-wei" or action without effort. It encourages individuals to let go of control and accept things as they come, rather than trying to force a certain outcome or make things happen your way.

- The Chinese philosophy of Daoism suggests that human beings should strive towards living in harmony with nature. This religious ideology emphasizes on the concept of harmony between man and nature as well as self-cultivation for achieving peace and balance within oneself.

- Ancient Chinese philosophies have survived for thousands of years and are still practiced today in various forms all over the world. They have been adapted and used in different cultures around the globe, making them one of the oldest surviving philosophical systems in history.

- The teachings of Confucianism form an integral part of Chinese culture, providing a moral code which has helped shape people's lives for centuries. Even today, it is often cited as one of the cornerstones of Chinese society and is viewed as a way to cultivate good character and maintain social order.

Medieval Philosophy

- Medieval philosophy was an era of intense philosophical discussion, debate and creative thought from the fifth to fifteenth centuries. This period saw many philosophers emerge who advanced philosophical ideas that would shape society today, such as Thomas Aquinas, Anselm of Canterbury and Augustine of Hippo. During this time, philosophy was used to interpret scripture and answer questions about human existence.

- Medieval philosophers often focused on understanding Aristotle's ideas and expanding upon them in their own writings. For example, Thomas Aquinas developed his famous five proofs for the existence of God based off of Aristotelian logic. At the same time, other thinkers like Duns Scotus reinterpreted Aristotle's views on morality and free will.

- Christianity played a major role in medieval philosophy, as it was used to explain and interpret scripture. Many philosophers interpreted Biblical passages as they related to questions of morality, existence and human nature. Augustine of Hippo wrote extensively on the relationship between faith and reason. He believed that faith can provide knowledge that reason alone cannot attain.

- Logic was a major component of the philosophical discussions during this period. Philosophers created logical frameworks for analyzing ideas such as causation, identity and necessity. The works of Peter Abelard, William of Ockham and John Buridan were important in developing logic-based approaches to philosophical questions.

- The debate between realists and nominalists was an important discussion within medieval philosophy. Realists believed that words correspond to real, objective things in the world, while nominalists argued that words do not necessarily refer to any particular thing outside of our own minds.

- Medieval philosophers often wrote about epistemology, or how we come to know something. Some thinkers believed in an innate knowledge of certain truths, while others thought that all knowledge must be acquired through experience and observation. Both Augustine and Aquinas wrote on this subject in detail.

- The debate over divine determinism was also a key issue during this time period. Determinism is the idea that everything has been predetermined by God and cannot be changed by humans, while some argued for free will as a way for humans to make their own decisions.

- Dualism, the belief that there are two distinct realms of existence: the physical and spiritual, was also a popular topic during this era. Augustine argued for the existence of two substances: body and soul, while Aquinas believed in three substances: body, soul and intellect.

- The philosophy of aesthetics was also discussed by medieval philosophers like Anselm of Canterbury. Anselm wrote about beauty in its many forms and how it can be appreciated without any external rewards or incentives. He saw beauty as an essential part of life that should be celebrated and cherished.

- In addition to writing on philosophical topics, some medieval philosophers wrote novels or stories with moral lessons. Geoffrey Chaucer is perhaps the most famous of these authors, writing tales like The Canterbury Tales and Troilus and Criseyde. These stories offered readers insight into the moral struggles that people experienced during this period.

RELIGION

- Did you know that the world's fastest growing religion is not Christianity, Islam or Judaism? It's actually an Indian philosophy called Hinduism which has over 1 billion followers worldwide. This ancient religion dates back to more than 5,000 years and is based on the teachings of various gods and goddesses such as Shiva and Krishna.

- While the majority of Christians follow Christianity, there are also lesser-known denominations like Coptic and Unitarian Universalists which have fewer followers. The Coptic Church is an ancient Egyptian sect that dates back to the time of Jesus Christ, where as Unitarian Universalists don't believe in any one god or faith and instead focus on the spiritual journey of human beings.

- Buddhism is a non-theistic religion that emerged in India about 2500 years ago and is based on the teachings of the historical Buddha Siddhartha Gautama. The most common form of Buddhism, Theravada, has over 150 million followers worldwide and focuses on meditation and mindfulness as ways to achieve inner peace and spiritual enlightenment.

- Did you know that in the Sikh religion, every male follower is required to wear a turban as part of their daily attire? This traditional headgear symbolizes equality, respect, courage and piety. The five symbols of faith -- kesh (uncut hair), kangha (comb), kara (iron bracelet), kirpan (sword) and rumaal (handkerchief) -- must also be worn by all Sikhs.

- Have you heard of the Rastafari movement? This religious movement is a form of Afro-Caribbean tradition which originated in Jamaica in the 1930s. It is based on the belief that former Ethiopian emperor Haile Selassie I, also known as Ras Tafari Makonnen, was a divine incarnation of God and its followers strive to live by the spiritual principles embodied in his teachings.

- Did you know that Shintoism is Japan's oldest religion? This faith is based on the worship of spirits known as kami, who inhabit all living things. Shintoism has over 3 million followers and its teachings center around nature, respect for ancestors and simplicity.

- Did you know that there are more than 12 million followers of Taoism worldwide? This ancient Chinese philosophy is rooted in the teachings of the Tao Te Ching and its main principle is to live in harmony with the Tao, or "the way", by following nature's laws. Taoism does not have any gods, but rather focuses on spiritual practices such as meditation and energy cultivation.

- Did you know that Zoroastrianism is one of the world's oldest monotheistic religions? This faith is rooted in the teachings of the ancient Persian prophet Zoroaster and its main belief is that there is only one God -- Ahura Mazda. There are currently around 200,000 followers of Zoroastrianism worldwide.

- Did you know that Baha'i is an independent world religion which has no connection to any other faith? Baha'i was founded in the 19th century by Mirza Husayn Ali Nuri and its teachings are based on the mystical unity of all religions. There are over 7 million followers of this religion spread across more than 200 countries.

- Did you know that in Hinduism, there are three major gods: Brahma, Vishnu and Shiva? Each of these gods represents a different aspect of creation and all three form a unified, divine trinity. Hindus believe that the cycle of death and rebirth is governed by these three deities and worshipping them brings the worshipper closer to moksha or spiritual liberation.

- Did you know that Confucianism is an ethical and philosophical system based on ancient Chinese teachings? It was founded by the philosopher Confucius in the 6th century BC and its main aim is to promote morality, justice and harmony. This faith has over 6 millions of followers worldwide and is widely practiced in many countries across East Asia.

- Did you know that Jainism is one of the world's oldest religions? This faith was founded by Mahavira in India in the 6th century BC and its main goal is to attain liberation from suffering through spiritual purity and non-violence or ahimsa. Jainism has over 4 million adherents worldwide and its teachings are based on five core principles or anuvratas.

- Did you know that the Druze faith is a monotheistic religion based on Islamic, Christian and Gnostic doctrines? This secretive religion was founded in Egypt in the 11th century AD and it is currently practiced by over 1 million people in the Middle East.

- Did you know that The Church of Jesus Christ of Latter-day Saints, also known as Mormonism, is a major world religion? It was founded in the 19th century by Joseph Smith and its main beliefs include scriptural authority, family values and baptism by immersion. There are currently around 16 million members of the Church worldwide.

- Did you know that Sikhism is a major world religion based on the teachings of Guru Nanak? This faith was founded in India in the 15th century and its main beliefs are centered around justice, equality and service to others. There are over 25 million Sikhs living in countries across the world.

- Did you know that Tenrikyo is a Japanese new religious movement that was founded in the 19th century? This faith is based on the teachings of Miki Nakayama and its main belief revolves around an omnipotent, loving parent figure known as God the Parent. Tenrikyo has around 2 million followers worldwide.

- Did you know that Shinto is an ancient religion with origins in Japan? It is based on animism and its main focus is to cultivate a relationship between humans and nature/the divine. There are around 4 million followers of Shintoism living in countries across the world, making it one of the most popular religions in Japan.

- Many religions around the world have similar stories and moral codes that tell us how to live well and care for each other. For example, Judaism, Christianity, and Islam all share the same story of Abraham's willingness to sacrifice his son.

- The Buddhist religion is based on teachings from Siddhartha Gautama, known as the "Buddha" or "Awakened One". He was born a prince in Nepal, but left his royal life to seek enlightenment and teach others about finding inner peace.

- Hindus believe that all living creatures have a soul and should be treated with respect. They revere cows, which symbolize care and nourishment, and believe that killing animals for food is wrong.

- In the Islamic faith, Muslims are expected to make a pilgrimage to Mecca at least once in their lifetime. This journey is called the Hajj and helps Muslims gain spiritual cleansing and come closer to Allah.

- Judaism has many different denominations, but all Jews follow the same basic laws from the Torah. These include honoring God, loving your neighbor, and keeping a moral and ethical code of conduct in order to live a righteous life.

- According to Taoism, humans should strive for harmony with nature by following "The Way". This involves respecting both yin and yang, the two opposing principles in life, and following the "middle path" between them.

- Christianity is based on Jesus Christ's teachings about love, compassion and forgiveness as well as his resurrection from death. Christians believe in one God who created heaven and earth, and that Jesus was sent to save mankind from sin.

- In the Sikh religion, Guru Nanak is revered as a messenger of God who taught his followers to live a life of service to others and devotion to God's will. They are also well known for their practice of wearing turbans, which is a sign of respect for God.

- Shintoism is a religion based on the belief in many different gods called kami, who are believed to live in nature and be present everywhere. This faith focuses on living harmoniously with nature and respecting ancestors by offering prayers and offerings.

- Zoroastrianism is an ancient Persian religion that originated with the teachings of Prophet Zoroaster. It involves following Ahura Mazda, the one true God and creator of all good things, and living in a way that brings righteousness into the world.

- Jainism is an ancient Indian religion that focuses on nonviolence towards all living beings and detachment from worldly desires. It also emphasizes meditation and austerities to help followers achieve spiritual enlightenment.

- Paganism is a polytheistic belief system that honors many different gods and goddesses from various cultures and regions around the world. Pagans focus on living in harmony with nature and celebrating the changing of the seasons.

- Baha'i faith originates from Persia and emphasizes spiritual unity among all humanity, regardless of race, gender, or social class. It also teaches that all religions have the same ultimate source and come from one God.

- Shintoism is an ancient Japanese faith that believes humans have a direct relationship with the gods. It emphasizes living in harmony with nature and honoring ancestors by offering prayers and offerings.

- Animism is the belief that all things, such as plants, animals, rocks, and even natural phenomena like thunder and lightning, have a spiritual essence. Animists believe that all of these things are connected and should be respected.

- All major religions emphasize compassion, kindness, respect for life and other moral virtues. The Islamic faith teaches believers to treat everyone with kindness, especially those who are vulnerable or in need. Similarly, Buddhists strive to live in harmony with nature and all living beings.

- Another similarity is that many of the world's religions encourage acts of charity and service. Hindus, for example, are taught to donate a portion of their income to charitable causes. In Christianity, Jesus taught his followers to serve others in need.

- Most religions have some concept of heaven and hell. For Christians, belief in an afterlife with rewards and punishments is integral to the faith. Hindus believe that after death one's soul is reincarnated based on one's actions in life.

- All religions have a code of ethics or moral guidelines for followers to live by. In Judaism, these are known as the Ten Commandments and can be found in the Hebrew Bible.
  Muslims adhere to the teachings of the Quran, while Buddhists follow a collection of ancient scriptures known as the Tripitaka, which include abstaining from killing and stealing.

- All major religions emphasize the importance of prayer or meditation as a way of connecting to God or a higher power. Indian spiritual traditions such as Hinduism and Buddhism have long emphasized the power of meditation to cultivate inner peace and balance.

- Most religions also maintain traditions that celebrate important events in their faith, such as religious holidays and festivals. Christians celebrate Easter to commemorate the resurrection of Jesus, and Muslims commemorate the end of Ramadan with a feast known as Eid al-Fitr.

- Many religions also emphasize fasting or abstinence from certain foods or activities for periods of time. In Islam, adherents fast during Ramadan to demonstrate their dedication to God and to cleanse their bodies and minds. In Christianity, fasting is often practiced during Lent to commemorate Jesus' forty days in the desert.

- Religions place great importance on stewardship of the environment. Hindus believe that nature is an aspect of God and should be respected accordingly, while Buddhists strive to live in harmony with all living beings.

- Almost all religions place great emphasis on rituals and ceremonies for special occasions. In Hinduism, the ceremonies surround birth, marriage and death. In Christianity, communion is regularly celebrated to commemorate the Last Supper of Jesus and his apostles.

- Jesus, Muhammad and Siddhartha Gautama (Buddha) were born in Jerusalem, Mecca, and Lumbini respectively. All three cities are located in the Middle East region and share a similar culture. Jesus was born to a Jewish family around 2000 years ago, while Muhammad and Siddhartha Gautama both belonged to a family of traders in the 6th and 5th centuries BC respectively.

- Jesus, Muhammad and Siddhartha Gautama are considered messengers of God and their teachings are seen as a divine gift to humanity. They all taught love, compassion, mercy, justice, humility and faith in one God or higher power. Jesus and Buddha were pacifists and preached non-violence, while Muhammad was a warrior aiming to spread justice.

- The stories of Jesus, Muhammad, and Siddhartha Gautama share certain common elements such as wanderings in search for spiritual enlightenment, the overcoming of temptations by evil forces, the healing of the sick and the development of a core group of followers.

- Jesus, Muhammad and Siddhartha Gautama all faced opposition from powerful authorities that tried to discredit their teachings and even assassinate them in some cases. Despite this, the three couldn't be silenced and continued preaching until their deaths.

- Even though they lived in different times and followed very different paths, Jesus, Muhammad and Siddhartha Gautama all experienced the same basic human emotions such as joy, sorrow, love and anger.

- All three religions ultimately aim to provide guidance to their followers on how to live a righteous life in accordance with God's will. This can be found in various religious texts, such as the Bible, Quran and Tipitaka.

- Jesus and Muhammad are believed to be resurrected after death in order to spread their message of love and peace. This is seen as a sign that they are truly divine messengers sent by God.

- Jesus, Muhammad and Siddhartha Gautama all believed that human beings have an immortal soul which survives death and is reborn again in the next life.

- All three religions believe that people should be judged by their actions and intentions rather than their social or economic status. They taught that everyone was equal before God, regardless of wealth or power.

- Jesus, Muhammad and Siddhartha Gautama all spoke out against oppression and injustice and advocated for the rights of people from all backgrounds.

- Many cultures around the world have creation stories that involve a godlike figure and/or divine being, often creating something out of nothing or ordering already existing things into organized form. For example, in Christianity and Judaism, God is said to have created the world in 6 days and rested on the seventh day.

- In some cultures, the creation of the world is seen as a process rather than an event. For example, in Hinduism, Brahma is said to have created the world out of himself and his thoughts over a long period of time.

- All the major world religions agree that the purpose of human life is a spiritual journey. This spiritual journey can involve achieving a connection with God, attaining inner peace, or reaching enlightenment.

- In some cultures, creation involves the separation of elements—light from dark and land from sea. For example, in Greek mythology, it was Chaos who separated the sky from the sea and created land.

- The creation stories of some cultures have a theme of overcoming chaos and bringing order to the world. In Hinduism, for example, Brahma is said to have brought order out of chaos by creating the four varnas (classes) in society.

- Many creation stories involve a female deity or divine being. Iranian and Indian religions, for example, feature the goddess Aditi as the mother of all gods who aided in the creation of the world.

- Some cultures use flood myths to explain how land came to be populated and why certain species exist. For example, in Christianity, Noah built an ark to save two of every animal species from a great flood. Similar myths are present in Mesopotamian culture, Nartive American Culture and Hinduism, among others.

- Many creation stories have a common theme of humans living in harmony with nature and the gods or divine beings that created them. For example, in Chinese mythology, the goddess Nuwa is said to have created humans out of clay and mud so that they could live in harmony with nature.

- Many religions feature elements of justice in their creation stories. For example, in Christianity, Adam and Eve are punished for disobeying God's command not to eat from the Tree of Knowledge.

- Creation stories may contain moral lessons or warnings about the consequences of human behavior. For example, in Greek mythology, Prometheus is punished by Zeus for giving fire to humans. In the Bible, God punishes Adam and Eve for disobeying him.

- Some cultures have creation stories that involve a struggle between two opposing forces—good and evil, light and dark, or order and chaos. In some Native American tribes like the Hopi, Cahuilla tribe, the Mohave, for example, the world was created out of the struggle between a crow and a coyote.

- Creation stories often include a sense of wonder and awe at the beauty of the world. In Hinduism, for example, Brahma is said to have created the world out of love and admiration for its beauty.

- Some cultures see creation as a continuing process, with new life being created all the time. For example, in some African tribes, birth is seen as a sacred and miraculous event, with each new child thought to be a reincarnation of an ancestor.

- Creation stories can also be used to explain the presence of natural disasters or hardships in the world. In some cultures, these events are seen as punishments from the gods or divine beings for disobeying their commands.

- Some cultures view creation as an act of self-sacrifice; that is, a sacrifice of the divine being's power or knowledge in order to create something new. In some versions of Christianity, for example, Jesus is said to have given up his life out of love for humanity.

- Many creation stories include themes of connectedness and unity between all things—humans, animals, plants and nature as a whole. This idea is expressed in the Hindu concept of Brahman, which views all things as both separate and part of a greater whole.

- Many creation stories emphasize the importance of gratitude to the divine being that created the world. This can be seen in Christianity, with Jesus's commandment to "Love thy neighbor as thyself," and in Hinduism, with the concept of bhakti (devotion) to Brahman.

- Many religions around the world believe in a Supreme Being or Creator, who is responsible for creating the universe and everything in it. For example,

Christianity believes that God created the world and all living things, while Hinduism believes that Brahma was responsible for this.

- Religions often teach that humans are given free will to make choices, meaning that humans have the ability to choose their own path and are held accountable for their actions.

- Religions often teach that there is an afterlife, or a life after death. For instance, Christianity teaches that those who have accepted Jesus Christ and his teachings will go to Heaven while Hindus believe in reincarnation, or being reborn into another form of life after death.

- Religions often have stories, myths, and legends associated with the creation of the world. For example, in Christianity the story of Adam and Eve is seen as an explanation for how human beings came to exist on Earth while in Hinduism there are many different stories about the creation of life such as that of Purusha and Prakriti (The sun and the flower)

- Religions have holidays that are celebrated to commemorate important events in the faith. For example, Christians celebrate Easter as a time of resurrection and renewal while Hindus observe Diwali as a festival of lights celebrating the victory of good over evil.

- Religions often believe in the concept of karma, or the idea that our actions have consequences. In other words, if we do something positive such as helping someone in need then good things will happen to us while negative actions will result in negative consequences.

- Religions often teach that humans should show respect for nature and the environment. For instance, Hinduism teaches that humans should appreciate the beauty of nature and take good care of it while Christianity encourages its followers to be stewards of the Earth.

- Religions often have rituals or ceremonies associated with them in which believers can participate. For example, Christians celebrate communion as a way to remember Jesus' sacrifice for humanity while Hindus observe puja, or the worship of deities through prayer and offerings.

- Religions often emphasize the importance of charity and giving back to those less fortunate. For example, Christianity focuses on giving back to the community and helping those in need while Buddhism encourages its followers to practice generosity by donating money or time to charitable causes.

- Religions often have symbols associated with them that are used to represent their faith and beliefs. For example, Christians use the cross as a symbol of their faith, while Hindus use symbols such as the Om and the swastika.

- Religions often have special places or locations that are associated with them such as churches, mosques, temples, or shrines. For example, Christians visit churches to worship God while Muslims go to mosques to pray.

- Religions often have certain rules and regulations that adherents must follow in order to remain faithful. For example, Christians practice abstinence from any sexual activity outside of marriage while Buddhists are expected to observe the Five Precepts which include not taking life, not stealing, abstaining from sexual misconduct, avoiding false speech, and refraining from intoxicants.

- Religions often have religious leaders or authorities who are responsible for providing guidance and instruction to the faithful. For example, Christians look to the Pope as their spiritual leader while Muslims look to Imams or scholars of Islam for guidance in matters of faith.

- Religion can bring people from different backgrounds and cultures together in a spirit of unity and harmony. For example, Christians from different denominations are able to come together at ecumenical conferences while members of different faiths can attend interfaith dialogues or conferences in order to learn more about each other's beliefs and practices.

- Religions often have music associated with them such as hymns for Christians or mantras for Buddhists. This type of music helps adherents to express their faith and spiritual devotion.

- Religion can provide comfort in times of suffering or sorrow. For example, Christians may turn to prayer as a source of solace while Hindus may seek refuge in meditation and reflection on the divine.

- Religion can be a source of strength and resilience during difficult times. For example, Muslims may turn to the Qur'an for inspiration and guidance while Buddhists may seek solace in their meditations and mindfulness practices.

- Religion can provide a sense of belonging by connecting people with a shared set of values, beliefs, and traditions. For example, Christians often find comfort in worshiping together as a congregation while Hindus may take part in festivals and celebrations with their fellow believers.

CULTURES

- The longest running religion in the world is Hinduism, which has been around for almost 4,000 years and has millions of followers across India and South Asia. Hindus believe in many gods and goddesses who are responsible for different aspects of life on Earth.

- Christianity is the most popular religion in the world with over 2.3 billion followers. It originated in the Middle East, and its main belief is that Jesus Christ was the son of God and died for our sins so that we can be saved from an eternity of punishment after death.

- The traditional Chinese culture believed in five elements: water, fire, earth, metal and wood. These elements were thought to be responsible for all things in the universe – from controlling the weather to influencing human personalities and emotions.

- Japan is known for its unique architecture with bright colors, steep roofs and intricate designs. The traditional Japanese style of architecture is called Shinto and emphasizes harmony between humans and nature - a concept that is still practiced today.

- In the Native American culture, there is a belief that animals are our teachers and guides, providing us with wisdom and guidance to help us through life's challenges.

- Arabs have a long tradition of storytelling passed down orally from generation to generation known as "Hikayat" which means "stories" in Arabic. These stories tell of heroic deeds and are used as a form of entertainment for children as well as adults.

- The ancient Egyptians believed that cats were sacred animals, and they even created mummified cat corpses to honor them after death.

- In many Mediterranean cultures it is considered very lucky to have a black cat walk in front of you because it is thought to bring good luck.

- In the Chinese culture, dragons are seen as powerful mythical creatures and symbols of strength. They are often used in art and architecture and can be found on many buildings throughout China.

- The traditional African culture believes that evil spirits exist throughout the world, and special rituals and dances - called "voodoo" - are performed to ward off these spirits and protect people from harm.

- The Aborigines of Australia have a rich culture that includes a variety of stories, music, art and ceremonies which are used to bring people closer together in their communities.

- The Burmese culture is heavily influenced by Buddhism, and it is thought that the practice of meditation can lead to enlightenment and inner peace.

- In India, cows are revered as sacred animals because of their association with Hindu god Krishna who was said to be a cow herder in his past life.

- In the Mexican culture, Dia de los Muertos (Day of the Dead) is celebrated annually to honor and remember deceased loved ones.

- The traditional Russian folk tales are filled with colorful characters and magical creatures that teach lessons about life and have entertained people for centuries.

- The Maasai tribe in Kenya and Tanzania practice a unique form of circumcision called Emuratare, which takes place when the children become teenagers. During this ceremony, the boys are circumcised and the girls' clitoris is pricked with a sharp object to cause minimal pain and avoid bleeding.

- In Greece, when a baby is born its father throws a plate onto the ground as a symbol of joy and a sign that the baby will have many suitors.

- In India, the Sadhu are holy men who live an ascetic life and travel the country in search of spiritual understanding. Some Sadhus refuse to cut their hair or nails, allowing them to grow very long over their lifetime.

- In Thailand, it is considered good luck to give a baby its first haircut at age one month. It is believed that this will bring long life and happiness to the child.

- In China, umbrellas are seen as symbols of bad luck and are traditionally not given as gifts.

- In Korea it is believed that burning incense will ward off evil spirits. This has led to the creation of many traditional rituals involving the burning of incense.

- In China, it is believed that red clothing will bring good luck and ward off evil spirits. This is why so many Chinese people wear red on their special occasions.

- In Egypt, it is traditional to hand out special eye-shaped jewelry and amulets, believed to ward off the "evil eye".

- In Morocco, it is considered good luck to eat a bowl of couscous on one's birthday as it is seen as a symbol of abundance and wealth.

- In Tibet, it is traditional to exchange khata cloths as a symbol of respect and good luck. The khata cloth is often blessed at a monastery first before being gifted.

- In the China, it is customary for parents to give their children coins known as "lucky money" on special occasions such as birthday or graduation.

- In Ireland, it is believed that throwing salt over one's shoulder will ward off bad luck and bring good luck. This practice is known as "throwing the devil away" and can be seen in many Irish households today.

- In Nigeria, it is believed that wearing certain beads will bring good luck and ward off evil spirits. These beads are known as "Owambe" and are usually made from clay, wood, or metal..

- In some areas of India, it is customary to exchange "bangles" as a symbol of friendship, loyalty, and good fortune.

- In Mexico, it is believed that carrying a rabbit's foot will bring good luck and protect the holder from harm.

- In Italy, it is seen as good luck to have someone throw rice over you on at your wedding.

- In East Asia, it is believed that carrying a lucky cat charm will bring good luck and attract wealth to its owner.

- In India, it is believed that keeping a Kalava string on you at all times can ward off bad luck and bring blessings to its holder.

- In Japan, it is believed that folding 1000 origami paper cranes will bring good luck, ward off illness and wishes becoming true.

- In Thailand, it is seen as good luck to give a newlywed couple nine coins in an envelope for wealth and security.

- In France, it is believed that carrying around a four-leaf clover will bring good luck.

- In China, it is customary to give a newborn baby a red string bracelet as it is believed to protect the child from bad luck and harm.

- In the Philippines, it is said that if you want good fortune, make sure to have your house facing east.

- In South Africa, it is believed that carrying a "dream catcher" around your neck will bring good luck and ward off bad dreams.

- The nomadic Tuareg people of North Africa wear blue robes, cheche scarves, and veils to protect themselves from the harsh Sahara desert sun.

- In China, a popular superstition is that the number 4 should be avoided as it sounds like death in Chinese culture.

- On St. Lucia's Day (December 13) in Sweden, boys dress up as "star boys" and carry stars on sticks while girls dress up as Lucia maids and wear white robes.

- In Spain, it's a custom to eat 12 grapes on New Year's Eve, one for each chime of the clock at midnight.

- In India, red is considered an auspicious color and is often worn during weddings or other special occasions.

- In Bulgaria, bread is very important to its culture and is presented on special occasions such as birthdays or weddings.

- In some African countries, animal skins are worn as clothing to show wealth and status in society.

- In Japan, it's a custom to take off your shoes before entering someone's home as a sign of respect.

- In Norway, the "konfirmasjon" is where 13-year-olds get confirmed to be an audult by a priest and receive gifts such as money and jewelry from their friends and family.

- Did you know that the Scottish wear kilts? The national dress of Scotland is called a kilt and is usually worn with pieces such as a sporran, sgian dubh, and tam o'shanter. The kilt comes in various colours, including green, red, blue and purple.

- In Japan, many people eat karashi-mentaiko (a marinated roe). It is a combination of spicy cod roe and sweet mayonnaise. This popular side dish is often served with rice or as an accompaniment to sushi.

- In India, Holi is a festival celebrated in the Spring that marks the beginning of the new harvest season. People throw colored powder and water at each other and celebrate with lots of dancing, music, and food!

- In Mexico, you can find mariachi bands who play traditional Mexican music in all kinds of venues from private events to public concerts. Their style features a combination of string instruments like violins and guitars, as well as drums, horns and sometimes even a harp.

- In Peru, you can observe the ancient tradition of the Qoyllur Riti festival every June. This is a religious celebration that includes ritual dances and ceremonies, culminating in a procession through the snow-capped mountains of the Andes.

- In China, the Mid-Autumn Festival is celebrated in September or October with an activity called 'mooncake hunting'. This involves children going out at night with paper lanterns to look for mooncakes, which are small cakes made of lotus paste and egg yolks.

- Did you know that in Israel, it's a tradition to give out small figurines of the prophet Elijah on the Jewish holiday, Passover? They are known as 'Elijah's cups' and they are filled with wine.

- Did you know that in Sweden, it is customary to give a bouquet of flowers on May Day? This is called 'mors dag', or Mother's Day and is celebrated by giving flowers to mothers, grandmothers and other female relatives.

- In Brazil, the Carnaval is held in late February or early March before Lent. This celebration includes parades, parties, music and dancing!

- Did you know that in Argentina, the tango is a popular dance? It originated in Buenos Aires and is known for its passionate moves and romantic lyrics.

- In Australia, didgeridoos are traditional musical instruments made from long hollow tree trunks or pieces of bamboo. They produce a low, rumbling sound and are sometimes used in ceremonies.

- In Indonesia, men play a game called 'Sepak Takraw' where they use their feet to kick a rattan ball over a net. It's like volleyball but with some differences such as points being scored for acrobatic moves!

- In Japan, it is considered disrespectful to blow your nose in public and you should never hand someone a business card upside-down as this is considered an insult. When given or receiving a business card, make sure to show respect by bowing slightly, handling delicately while holding it with two hands, on the right side, and making eye contact.

- In India, it is considered rude to show the soles of your feet. When sitting in front of someone, make sure to keep them off the floor and instead cross your legs or tuck them away under you.

- In Mexico, it is offensive to refuse food when offered by a host. It's important to remember that hospitality is taken seriously in Mexico, and politely asking for a smaller portion is considered polite.

- In Korea, it is not acceptable to pour your own drink or eat before others have started eating. Also, don't point with your chopsticks as this is seen as impolite and should be avoided.

- In Thailand, it is considered disrespectful to touch someone on the head and women should never be touched by men. Also, when entering a temple or shrine, make sure to wear appropriate clothing (no shorts or tank tops).

- In Turkey, it is considered rude to leave food on your plate after eating, and you should always finish what you are served.

- In Saudi Arabia, it is not OK for women to drive and they should always be accompanied by a male family member when traveling outside the home. Also, it's important to avoid public displays of affection as this is considered inappropriate in their culture.

- In China, it's important to avoid touching anyone, especially children. It is also best to not talk with your hands in their presence as this is seen as disrespectful.

- In Italy, it's important to remember to say "grazie" (thank you) after receiving something and not touch or point at religious images.

SCIENCE

- The speed of light is 299,792,458 m/s! That's faster than any other speed known to man. If you could travel the same speed as light, you would be able to go around the world 7 and a half times in one second!

- The average adult human body contains billions of atoms. Every atom in your body is billions of years old and comes from ancient stars that have long since died!

- The human brain is incredibly powerful, but it only uses about 20 watts of energy while you're awake – that's the same amount of energy as a lightbulb!

- The brain is made up of about 86 billion neurons, which are like tiny switches that control the flow of electricity in our bodies.

- Your heart beats around 100,000 times a day and pumps about 8,000 liters of blood – that's enough to fill an Olympic swimming pool in a month!

- Earth is constantly spinning around its axis at a speed of 1,000 mph – that's faster than the speed of sound (767 mph)!

- The air you breathe contains about 78% nitrogen, 21% oxygen and other trace gases like carbon dioxide.

- The average temperature on Earth is 57°F (14°C). In the deepest parts of the ocean, it can be as cold as -2°F (-19°C)!

- Clouds form when tiny water droplets or ice crystals join together to make bigger droplets. When enough droplets join together, a cloud is born!

- It is thought that there are approximately 8.7 million species of plants and animals existing on the planet today, but only 1.2 million of these have been officially identified and scientifically catalogued - most of which being insects. This means that much of the earth's biota still remains a mystery!

- It is believed that there are more than 7 million animal species in the world, with 1.5 million of them having been identified so far. Most of these classified species belong to the insect family, but there are also a variety of other animals including fish, mammals and birds

- The tallest mountain on Earth is Mount Everest, which stands at an incredible 8,848 meters (29,029 feet) above sea level.

- The Sun is about 4.5 billion years old and will keep burning for another 5 billion years before it dies out completely!

- The average person sheds about 1.5 million skin cells every day – that's about the same weight as a small apple!

- The human body contains 206 bones, and our skeleton changes shape as we grow from children to adults. Babies are actually born with more than 300 bones, but as they age some of the smaller bones fuse together.

- The average person sheds about 1.5 million skin cells every day – that's about the same weight as a small apple!

- The Milky Way galaxy is estimated to be 100,000 light years across! That means if you were able to travel at the speed of light it would take you 100,000 years to get from one side of the Milky Way to the other.

- You've probably heard that the Earth is round, but did you know that it is actually an oblate spheroid? That means it's a bit flattened at the top and bottom!

- The Earth rotates around its axis once every 24 hours, which is why we have day and night cycles. This rotation also causes the seasons to change throughout the year as the Earth moves around the Sun.

- There are 8 planets in our Solar System: Mercury, Venus, Earth, Mars, Jupiter, Saturn, Uranus and Neptune. Plus there are dwarf planets like Pluto!

- The Moon is actually moving away from the Earth at a rate of about 1.6 inches per year – that mayd the Sun.

- The average adult human body contains about 5 liters of blood! Blood helps carry oxygen and other important nutrients throughout our bodies.

- Our bones are made from a material called calcium phosphate, which also makes up the shells of certain animals such as crabs, lobsters and snails.

- Blood vessels are like tiny tube-shaped highways that carry blood throughout our bodies. They can be as small as 2 micrometers in size!

- The Earth is covered in about 70% water. Over 96% of this water can be found in oceans.

- The speed of light is 186,282 miles per second – that's about 671 million miles per hour!

- Every second, the Sun produces enough energy to power every home on Earth for 500,000 years!

- A single lightning bolt contains enough energy to power a 60-watt light bulb for 6 months.

- A rainbow is one of nature's most colorful displays, and it's caused by the refraction of sunlight through tiny water droplets in the atmosphere.

- An apple can float because it is filled with air pockets that help make it less dense than water.

- Your fingerprints are completely unique and can't be changed or erased!

- The Earth has an inner core made of solid iron and nickel that is about the same temperature as the surface of the Sun!

- A single raindrop can travel up to 25 miles per hour, depending on the wind!

- The average person blinks about 15 times per minute, or about 10 million times each year!

- There are 1,000 different species of ants living on every continent except Antarctica. In total, it is believed that there are 12,000 different species on ants on earth.

- The human eye can detect around 1 million different colors and shades!

- Red is the first color that babies can recognize and it's also the most attractive color to them!

- The human eyeball is about the same size as a ping pong ball and weighs about 0.25 ounces. It's made of three main layers: sclera (the white part), choroid (the middle layer) and retina (the inner layer). All these layers work together to help you see by processing light and sending signals to the brain.

- Did you know that the human tongue is made up of eight different muscles, which help us to speak, taste and swallow?

- Every single one of your fingertips has about 3 thousands sweat glands per square inch of skin — more than any other part of your body! Sweat helps cool our bodies down when we're hot.

- The human nose can remember up to 50,000 different smells — that's more than any other sense!

- Human skin is the largest organ in our body — it's made up of over 15% of our total body weight. It's also waterproof, breathable and helps regulate our body temperature.

- The human liver is one of the most important organs in our bodies — it filters toxins from our blood, stores energy and regulates hormones. It's the only organ in the body that can regenerate itself when damaged!

- Did you know that the human body produces 3.8 million new cells every second? Approximately 86% are blood cells, 14% epithelial cells.

- Your bones are strong but surprisingly lightweight — if all of your bones were put together, they'd only weigh around 6-8 pounds.

- The human body has tons of different types of cells, but the smallest cell is the red blood cell. It's about 7-8 micrometres in diameter — that's about 1/1000th of an inch!

- Your lungs are made up of over 300 million tiny air sacs called alveoli. They take oxygen from the air we breathe and pass it into our bloodstream.

- Your body has a built-in cooling system — the sweat glands! When your body temperature starts to rise, these glands secrete sweat which helps cool you down.

- The human kidney is an amazing organ — it filters about 200 quarts of blood each day, removing waste and extra water from the body. This quantity is enough to fill a large bathtub.

- The human spine is made up of 33 separate bones called vertebrae which are stacked one on top of the other and connected by muscles and ligaments. This "stack" helps us stand upright and move.

- Your brain is the control center for your body — it sends messages all over your body to tell it what to do, whether that's wiggling your toes, digesting food or blinking your eyes!

- Human hair grows an average of 1/2 inch per month. It's also the fastest growing tissue in the body!

- The human brain can generate up to 23 watts of power when fully engaged – enough energy to light a light bulb! On average, the brain uses around 20% of the body's total energy expenditure and is capable of generating an impressive amount of electricity. All this electricity is used for complex tasks such as thinking, learning and remembering.

- It is estimated that each person can generate up to 70,000 thoughts per day – that's a lot of ideas!

- The human brain is constantly changing and adapting to its environment. It's called neuroplasticity – the ability of the brain to reorganize itself by forming new neural connections throughout life. This means that we can learn new skills, build memories and make new connections as we age.

- The human brain is capable of storing up to 2.5 petabytes of information – equivalent to the data contained in about 500 billion pages of written text. That's an incredible amount of information for such a small organ, and it could store even more if we were able to tap into its full potential.

- The human brain can process visuals 60,000 times faster than text! This is why visuals are so important in learning and understanding new concepts– they provide an easier way to make connections and remember information.

- Humans use only 5% of their brains – this myth has been debunked many times over, but it's still widely believed. In fact, the human brain uses 100% of its capacity, no matter what we're doing!

- Our brains are constantly producing new neurons – in fact, it's estimated that we create around 700 new neurons every day! This process is called neurogenesis and helps us to form new memories and associations.

- The human brain can process as much information in one second as a supercomputer can process in one day! This is largely due to the incredible speed at which our brains transmit electrical signals, allowing us to think quickly and make decisions.

- The human brain has four main lobes – the frontal lobe, temporal lobe, occipital lobe and parietal lobe. Each of these lobes is responsible for different functions, such as motor control, language, vision and hearing.

- The human brain is capable of multitasking – it can handle several tasks at once and switch between them quickly and efficiently. This incredible ability allows us to do more with our time and make better use of our cognitive resources.

- The human brain has an incredible ability to store information – it can recall vast amounts of information, even years after it was learned. This is thanks to the connections formed between neurons which help us to recall memories and information quickly and accurately.

- The human brain can learn new skills at any age – even in our later years, our brains can still form new neural connections and pick up new skills. This means that it's never too late to learn a new language or master a new hobby.

ANIMALS

- Crows are able to recognize human faces, remember them and can even hold grudges against people who have wronged them! Not only do crows remember faces of people who have threatened or scared them, but they also alert other crows to be careful around those people. Additionally, crows have been known to seek out revenge against people who have wronged them.

- Bald eagles are incredibly strong, they can carry up 4 or 5 pounds weight.

- Sloths are so slow that they only move around 41 yards in a day! Despite this slow pace, sloths are surprisingly skilled swimmers, however they rarely leave the safety of their trees. The reason for their sluggish pace is because its how they conserve energy since their diet consists primarily of leaves.

- Cheetahs can run up to 70 mph and can accelerate from 0 to 60 mph in just three seconds! This makes them one of the fastest animals on land.

- Elephants can recognize themselves in a mirror! This is an incredibly rare trait among animals, as most creatures do not have the cognitive abilities to understand what they are seeing in a reflection. Elephants are one of the few species who can identify their own reflections and use it to inspect areas that may be difficult to reach otherwise.

- Elephants have an extremely long gestation period of 22 months, longer than any other mammal!

- Sharks can actually go into a trance like state when they are flipped upside down! This unique behavior is known as tonic immobility, and it occurs when sharks are placed in a vulnerable position and rendered motionless. Researchers believe this behavior is an evolutionary adaptation used by sharks to protect themselves from predators.

- The toad's skin is so sticky, it can even pick up small stones.

- Bats can fly up to speeds of 60 mph and can detect the movement of prey by using sound waves! To do this, bats release a high-pitched sound that bounces off objects in its environment and returns as an echo which tells them where the prey is located. This process is known as echolocation.

- Penguins are excellent swimmers and can reach speeds of up to 25 mph under the water.

- Penguins have an incredibly thick layer of feathers, which helps them keep warm in icy cold waters! The feathers on a penguin's body are arranged to be waterproof and trap air close to their skin, which keeps them insulated from the frigid temperatures. Additionally, penguins can even drink saltwater due to special glands which filter out the salt.

- Aardvarks are nocturnal animals that mostly feed on ants and termites! They have long snouts which they use to easily suck up their prey.

- Owls can turn their heads a full 270 degrees, which is more than twice as much as humans! This incredible flexibility is thanks to the special structure of owl's necks, which contain 14 vertebrae compared to humans who only have 7 vertebrae. Additionally, owls are able to see in almost complete darkness which helps them hunt for prey.

- The star-nosed mole has the most sensitive nose in the animal kingdom and can detect food with its tentacles at an incredible speed of 8 milliseconds! The animal has about 100,000 nerves to make it possible.

- Albatrosses are some of the longest living birds on Earth, with a lifespan of up to 60 years! These birds stand out from other species due to their impressive wingspan of up to 11 feet, allowing them to soar through the air without flapping their wings for hours at a time. Albatrosses are also capable of flying over long distances of up to 10,000 miles in a single journey!

- The Scottish Wildcat is the only species of wild cat native to the British Isles and is considered an endangered species as it gets often hybridized with domestic cats.

- Snakes have two sets of eyelids – an upper and lower lid! The unique structure of their eyes allows them to see both day and night, although they do not have the ability to focus on images like humans do. Snakes also have a fascinating feature known as "heat pits" which allow them to detect warm-blooded prey in the dark.

- The Australian emu can run up to 31 mph and is the second-fastest bird in the world!

- Polar bears have special fur that is made up of hollow tubes, which help keep them stay warm! The air pockets inside the fur absorb the heat from their body, keeping them insulated even in the coldest of temperatures. Additionally, they have two layers of fur – an outer layer which is transparent and helps to block out light, and an inner layer which contains extra air pockets for insulation.

- The African elephant is the biggest land animal in the world, weighing up to 11 tons and reaching heights of 13 feet! They have an incredibly long life span, living up to 70 years in the wild! Elephants also communicate using sound frequencies at such low levels, they are only detectable by other elephants.

- Owls have incredible vision and it is estimated that they can see 10-80 times better than humans in low light conditions.

- The Giant Pacific octopus is one of the largest species of octopus in the world, with an average arm span of 16 feet and a weight reaching up to 40 pounds! They have three hearts, nine brains, and blue blood! Octopuses are also able to change color in order to camouflage themselves or communicate with other octopuses.

- Beavers are very industrious animals and build dams made of sticks and mud that can be up to 12 feet high!

- The King Cobra is the longest venomous snake in the world, reaching lengths of up to 18 feet! They have an impressive speed of 12 mph and can raise one-third of their body off the ground when threatened! King cobras also have a special ability to find their prey even in complete darkness, thanks to their heat-sensing "pits".

- The komodo dragon is the largest lizard in the world and can grow up to 10 feet long!

- Sharks have a very advanced sense of smell, which allows them to detect even small traces of blood from miles away.

- The Gharial is one of the most distinctive species of crocodile, known for its long thin snout and sharp teeth! They mainly live in the rivers of India and Nepal, and can reach lengths of up to 20 feet! Gharials also have special webbed feet which help them swim faster and catch their prey more easily.

- The Blue Whale is the largest mammal that has ever lived, weighing up to 200 tons and reaching lengths of up to 100 feet! They feed on tiny shrimp-like creatures called krill, which they filter out of the ocean water with their huge mouths! Blue Whales also communicate with each other through low frequency sounds that can travel up to 500 miles away.

- African wild dogs are extremely social animals and live in large packs with a very complex social structure.

- The African Wild Dog is one of the most endangered species on Earth, with an estimated population of only 6,600! They are known for their unique spotted coats, which help to camouflage them in the grass. African Wild Dogs also have large ears that help them to hear predators and prey from far away.

- The Pufferfish is one of the most poisonous fish in the world, containing a toxin that can kill a human in minutes! Despite their dangerous nature, they are also incredibly cute, with big eyes and a playful personality. Pufferfish also have the ability to inflate their bodies up to 3 times their size when threatened by predators. Pufferfish are so venomous that one of them could kills 30 adult humans.

- The Asian Elephant is slightly smaller than its African counterpart, but still one of the most impressive creatures on the planet! They have the amazing ability to remember routes, landmarks and even individual trees from years before. Asian

Elephants also have a special layer of skin which is twice as thick as human skin, made up of two layers – an outer layer which is transparent and helps to block out light, and an inner layer which contains extra air pockets for insulation.

- The giant panda is the only bear species that eats primarily bamboo and can consume up to 80 pounds of it in one day!

- The Vampire Squid is a mysterious creature that lives in the depths of the ocean, where there is no light! It has special photophores on its tentacles which give off a blue, glow-in-the-dark effect to attract prey. The Vampire Squid also has an incredible defense mechanism: it can release a cloud of black ink when threatened, which blocks out the light and confuses predators!

- The Honey Badger is an incredibly tough, fearless creature that has no natural enemies! It has a thick layer of fur to protect it from stings and bites, as well as razor sharp claws and teeth that allow it to dig into burrows and hunt for food. Honey Badgers also have incredibly strong jaws which can bite through the toughest of hides with ease!

- The Axolotl is a species of salamander that lives in lakes and rivers in Mexico, and never grows past 9 inches in length! It has unique feathery gills on both sides of its head, which filter oxygen out of the water. Axolotls also have a special ability to regenerate their body parts if they become injured or damaged!

- The Red Fox is one of the most recognizable animals on Earth, with its bright orange fur and pointed ears! They are incredibly adaptable, able to survive in a wide range of habitats, including deserts and forests. Red Foxes also have incredible hearing, which allows them to detect the faintest of noises from far away!

- The Grolar Bear is a hybrid between a Polar Bear and a Brown Bear, created when they mate in the wild! They are incredibly rare animals, but are growing in number due to the changing climate. Grolar Bears also have a special thick layer of fur, which helps to keep them warm and insulated in the coldest temperatures.

- The Honey Bee is one of the most important pollinators on the planet, responsible for helping to create food sources for humans and animals alike! They have special hairy bodies which help them to collect pollen and nectar from flowers, and bristles on their legs which allow them to carry it back to the hive.

- Bats are the only mammals that can truly fly! They use echolocation to find their way around in the dark.

- The Electric Eel is one of the most dangerous animals in the world, as it has the ability to produce an electric shock of up to 860 volts! Despite this, they are actually quite peaceful and shy creatures, preferring to hide in dark corners rather than attack. Electric Eels also have special organs which allow them to sense the electrical fields of their prey from far away!

- The Royal Bengal Tiger is one of the most majestic animals on Earth, with its bright orange and black stripes! They are also incredibly powerful creatures, able to leap up to 20 feet when hunting prey. Royal Bengal Tigers also have a special sense of smell which allows them to detect prey from miles away!

- The pronghorn is one of the fastest land animals on Earth and can reach speeds up to 60 mph while running! Its amazing speed comes from a combination of powerful leg muscles, large lungs and specialized hooves.

- The King Cobra is one of the most feared snakes in the world, as it has a deadly venom which can kill its prey within minutes! However, they are actually quite shy and timid creatures, preferring to stay away from humans. King Cobras also have incredibly long fangs which can reach up to 3 inches in length!

- The Giant Tortoise is one of the longest-living animals on Earth, with some specimens living for over 100 years! They have incredibly thick shells which protect them from predators, as well as air pockets for insulation. Giant Tortoises also have a special ability to store water in their stomachs, allowing them to survive in the most arid of climates!

- Giraffes can go for up to 3 weeks without drinking water. They get most of their moisture from the plants they eat which makes it possible for them to live in deserts and other dry places.

- The Octopus is one of the most intelligent animals in the ocean, able to solve puzzles and even mimic other creatures! They have incredible camouflage abilities, changing their skin colour and texture to blend into the background. Octopuses also have special suckers on their tentacles which allow them to grip onto objects with ease!

- Certain species of jellyfish can be immortal if not eaten by predators or other hazards of the environment. The jellyfish Turritopsis dohrnii can transform back into a juvenile stage and cycle again through adulthood, making it potentially immortal.

- If a bee lands on you, the best thing to do is stay still until it flies away - because if you swat at it, it may leave behind its stinger and die. Bees are essential pollinators in many ecosystems and play an important role in keeping them healthy.

- The Venus flytrap is the only plant known to catch and eat animals as prey. Its leaves can snap shut on unsuspecting insects, trapping them until they are digested with digestive enzymes produced by the plant itself.

- The Amazon rainforest is home to a dizzying array of unique species, with an estimated 390 billion individual trees divided into 16,000 different species. This makes it one of the most biodiverse places on the planet.

- Some mushrooms have even been found to be able to digest plastic and turn it into nourishment for itself. The mushroom species Pestalotiopsis microspora was discovered to be able to feed on polyurethane, a type of plastic used in many consumer items.

- Some organisms living in hydrothermal vents at the bottom of the ocean lack eyes as they live in total darkness so far from the sun's rays. Yet they can still detect their environment using chemosynthesis, a process that uses chemicals in the water to make energy.

- The Sahara desert is so large and dry it can be seen from space. It covers an area of 3.5 million square miles (9 million sq km) and stretches across 11 countries in North Africa – making it almost as big as the United States.

- The Sargasso Sea, located in the middle of the North Atlantic ocean, is home to a variety of species that go through their entire life cycle without ever touching land. It's also known for its thick mats of floating seaweed, which can be 100 feet deep in some places.

- The ocean is home to a variety of creatures that can produce their own light, known as bioluminescence. Some marine species use this light for defense, communication, and even mating rituals.

- The Atacama Desert in Chile is so dry and barren that some areas have never seen rain, making it one of the driest places on earth. Yet, there are still some species that have adapted to survive in this extreme climate.

- The Great Barrier Reef is the largest living structure on Earth and can be seen from space. It's home to an incredible diversity of marine life, including over 1,500 species of fish, 400 species of coral and 4,000 kinds of mollusks.

- The Amazon River is the longest river in the world and has more water than any other river on Earth. Its basin covers over 2 million square miles (5 million sq km) making it larger than the United States.

- The Earth's atmosphere is made up of mostly nitrogen (78%) and oxygen (21%). This mix of gases, along with trace amounts of other elements, creates the perfect environment for life as we know it.

- The universe contains billions of galaxies, each one containing millions or even billions of stars. One galaxy alone – the Milky Way – is estimated to contain anywhere from 100 to 400 billion stars.

- The universe is expanding at an ever-increasing rate, meaning that the farther away something is in space, the faster it appears to be moving away from us. This phenomenon has been described by scientists as "the Hubble flow".

- The Rafflesia arnoldii is the largest flower in the world and can reach up to 3 feet in diameter and weigh up to 15 pounds. It is native to Sumatra, Indonesia, and emits a smell similar to that of rotting flesh, which attracts insects for pollination.

- The oldest living tree in the world is a bristlecone pine located in the White Mountains of California. It is estimated to be 5,065 years old and still growing!

- The Australian eucalyptus deglupta tree can grow up to 90 meters tall and its trunk can measure up to 7 meters in circumference. Its leaves can change color from green to yellow, pink and purple.

- The common garden snail is the slowest moving land animal in the world, with a speed of 0.03 mph or 0.048 km/h.

- The Eastern Lubber grasshopper (Romalea microptera) is the largest grasshopper in America and can measure up to 5 inches long.

- The Venus flytrap (Dionaea muscipula) is a carnivorous plant that can eat insects, spiders and even arachnids!

- The Ginkgo tree (Ginkgo biloba) is one of the oldest living tree species in the world, with records of its existence from 200 million years ago.

- The longest living animal on Earth is the ocean quahog, a type of clam that can live up to 500 years.

- The Amborella trichopoda tree is the closest living relative of all flowering plants and has remained unchanged since its ancestors appeared 140 million years ago.

- The common banana plant produces a single stem with multiple shoots, each of which can grow up to 25 feet tall.

- The Australian eucalyptus deglupta, commonly known as the Rainbow Gum tree, is one of the most colorful trees in the world due to its multi-colored bark.

- The African baobab tree (Adansonia digitata) can grow up to 25 meters tall and its trunk can measure up to 10 meters in circumference – making it one of the most iconic trees on the continent.

- The fastest growing plant in the world is the giant bamboos, which can grow up to one meter per day.

- The world's tallest tree is a coast redwood named Hyperion and stands at 115.5 meters tall, as measured in 2006.

- The world's largest seed is the coco de mer, the seed of a palm tree native to the Seychelles. It can weigh up to 18-25 kg and measure up to 30 cm in diameter!

- The Victoria Amazonica water lily has one of the the world's largest flower and can measure up to 3 meter in diameter.

- The Mountain Gorilla (Gorilla beringei) is the world's largest primate, with males standing up to 1.8 meters tall (5 ft 6 In) and weighing up to 225 kg. The largest gorilla ever recorded in 1938 and was 1.95 meters (6 ft 5 ln).

INVENTIONS

- The earliest wheels in prehistoric times were used for pottery and not for transport, which came centuries later. Wheels were also used by Egyptians to create chariots, which allowed them to move faster and more efficiently on the battlefield. Finally, the wheel was a major contributor to early technological advancements such as irrigation systems and pulley systems.

- Fire is believed to have been first discovered by Homo erectus about 200,000 years ago, and it was used for cooking and warmth. It has also been a major factor in human evolution through its use as an energy source and its importance in the development of agriculture. Additionally, fire was a key element of the industrial revolution, enabling the manufacturing of steel and other metals.

- Early forms of writing appeared in Egypt around 3200 BC, and were used for both personal record keeping and communication between individuals or groups. Later, writing was instrumental in the spread of knowledge throughout early society, and is still a key element today in books, newspapers, and other forms of communication. Writing also helped create a more organized society, as it allowed for laws to be documented and for better preservation of history.

- The invention of the printing press in 1450 AD by German blacksmith Johannes Gutenberg marked a turning point in human history. It was the first time that written texts could be reproduced en masse, which allowed for the spread of knowledge and ideas much faster than before. This invention also led to a major increase in literacy rates throughout Europe as books could now be made more cheaply and quickly.

- The discovery of electricity by Englishman William Gilbert in 1600 marked a pivotal moment in human history. Electricity changed the way we work, play and think. Electricity powered the industrial revolution with its introduction of machinery, automation and power tools. It also changed our lives in the home with electric lights, appliances, televisions and computers.

- The invention of the steam engine by James Watt in 1764 allowed for an increase in production as machines could be powered by steam instead of human labor. It also enabled the transportation of goods over longer distances and heavier loads, as ships, trains and automobiles could be powered with steam. This invention also allowed for increased exploration of previously inaccessible areas such as oceans and mountains.

- The first computer was invented in the 1940s, and it was named ENIAC (Electronic Numerical Integrator and Computer). It was a massive machine that contained over 18,000 vacuum tubes, 70,000 resistors, 10,000 capacitors, and 6,000 switches—all of which made it the largest and most powerful computer of its time.

- The first lightbulb was created by Thomas Edison in 1879, and it changed the way people lived forever. It used a filament made from carbonized bamboo that glowed when electricity passed through it, providing an efficient and reliable source of light that could last for up to 1,200 hours.

- The first automobile was invented by Karl Benz in 1885 and consisted of three wheels, an engine, and a simple transmission system. This vehicle changed transportation and the way people lived their lives in unprecedented ways, making it easier to travel long distances quickly and cheaply.

- The concept for radio was first proposed by James Clerk Maxwell in 1873 and was a way to transmit information without the need for wires. Guglielmo Marconi developed the first practical radio system in 1895, which used electromagnetic waves to send messages over long distances.

- The world's first nuclear reactor was built in 1942 by scientists at the University of Chicago. This reactor, called the Chicago Pile-1 (CP-1), was the first man-made device to produce and sustain a nuclear chain reaction. It provided an invaluable source of information for further research into nuclear energy and atomic weapons.

- The world's first television was invented in 1926 by Scottish-born engineer John Logie Baird. It used a spinning disk with small holes in it to scan images, which were then broadcast and received by a special receiver. This invention revolutionized the way people consume media, providing them with entertainment, news, and educational content on demand.

- The transistor was invented by John Bardeen, Walter Brattain and William Shockley in 1947. This invention revolutionized electronics, making it possible to produce incredibly small and efficient electronic devices such as computers, radios and televisions. It changed the way people interact with technology and paved the way for the modern digital age.

- The Internet was invented in 1969 by ARPANET, a project of the U.S. Defense Department's Advanced Research Projects Agency (ARPA). It revolutionized communication and allowed for near-instant global access to information and resources. Today, more than 4 billion people use the Internet around the world, with over 2 billion websites and trillions of emails sent every day.

- The World Wide Web (WWW) was invented in 1989 by British computer scientist, Tim Berners-Lee. It works in conjunction with the Internet to provide a platform for users to access information quickly and easily from anywhere in the world.

- Social media was invented in 1997 by a team at Six Degrees and is now one of the most popular activities on the Internet. It has changed how people stay connected with friends, family and acquaintances around the world, allowing them to easily share messages, photos and videos. Today, over 2 billion people are active on social media each month.

- The first smartphone was invented in 1992 by IBM and BellSouth as the Simon Personal Communicator. Though it wasn't a true "smartphone," it provided users with the ability to access email, browse the Internet, and do other tasks with a cellular device. The modern smartphone was born in 2007 when Apple released the first iPhone and changed how people use technology for communication and entertainment. Today, over 3 billion people own smartphones around the world.

- The Global Positioning System (GPS) was developed by the U.S. Department of Defense in 1973 to provide accurate navigation and location services for military personnel. It has since been made available to the public and is now used by over 1 billion people around the world to quickly determine their exact location and get directions from one place to another.

- The first 3D printing machine was invented in 1983 by Chuck Hull and was commercially available in the late 90s. It revolutionized commercial manufacturing, allowing users to quickly and easily create objects from raw materials using digital designs stored on a computer. Today, 3D printing is used by people around the world for a variety of different applications.

- Wi-Fi technology was invented in 1971 but only became widely available in the late 90s. It revolutionized communication, allowing people to easily access the internet wirelessly from anywhere in their homes or offices. Today, Wi-Fi is available in over 400 million public hotspots around the world and is used by more than 3 billion people worldwide.

- Voice recognition technology was developed by Bell Laboratories in 1952 and was used in the early 2000s to understand spoken commands and transcribe them into text. Today, it is widely available on computers, smartphones and other devices and used by over 1 billion people around the world to quickly search for information, control their device's settings and more.

- The first digital camera was invented in 1975 by Steven Sasson at Kodak but only became widely available to the public in the early 2000s. It changed how people take and store photos, allowing them to quickly snap pictures and share them with friends and family around the world. Today, over 1 billion digital cameras are used by people every day for personal photography needs.

SCIENTISTS

- Galileo Galilei is considered the father of modern physics and observational astronomy. He was an Italian polymath who made pioneering observations of nature with long-lasting consequences for the study of science. His discoveries revolutionized astronomy, physics and mathematics. He made a number of groundbreaking discoveries about the universe. He is credited with developing the first telescope and discovering four moons around Jupiter, which provided evidence that the Earth is not the center of the universe. He also formulated the law of inertia, which states that objects in motion will stay in motion unless acted upon by an external force.

- Albert Einstein is renowned as one of the most influential scientists in human history. He developed the special theory of relativity and the general theory of relativity, which laid the framework for modern physics. He also received a Nobel Prize in Physics in 1921 for his work on theoretical physics.

- Isaac Newton is considered one of the most influential scientists ever and was an English polymath who made important contributions to mathematics, optics and physics. He formulated the law of gravity, which explains why objects fall to the ground, and developed calculus, a mathematical language that describes how things move in the universe.

- Michael Faraday was an English chemist and physicist who discovered electromagnetic induction, which showed how electricity could be generated from magnetism. He also devised the first electric motor and discovered the laws of electrolysis, which allowed for the production of large amounts of electricity.

- Niels Bohr was a Danish physicist who made significant contributions to quantum mechanics and atomic structure. He is known for proposing the wave-particle duality theory, which states that light can be both a particle and a wave. He was awarded the Nobel Prize in Physics in 1922 for his work on atomic structure and radiation.

- Stephen Hawking was an English theoretical physicist, cosmologist and author who made groundbreaking discoveries about black holes, gravitational waves and quantum theory. One of his most famous works is A Brief History of Time, which contains many of his theories and became a best-seller.

- Ernest Rutherford was a New Zealand physicist who discovered the structure of atoms. He proposed the Rutherford model, which states that atoms are composed of a small, positively charged nucleus surrounded by negatively charged electrons in orbit around it. This model is still used today to explain atomic structure.

- J.J. Thomson was an English physicist who discovered the electron and developed a mathematical model to explain how atoms are composed of negatively charged particles called electrons, which are embedded in a sea of positive charge. He was awarded the Nobel Prize in Physics in 1906 for his discoveries about matter and radiation.

- Marie Curie was a Polish physicist and chemist who discovered the elements radium and polonium. She is credited with introducing radiation in medicine, which led to the development of X-ray machines and treatments for cancer. She also became the first woman to ever win a Nobel Prize in Physics in 1903.

- James Clerk Maxwell was a Scottish mathematician and physicist who developed a mathematical model to explain electricity, magnetism and light. His work provided the foundation for modern physics and he is credited with formulating the four Maxwell's equations, which describe how electric and magnetic fields interact with each other.

- Werner Heisenberg was a German theoretical physicist who made significant contributions to quantum mechanics. He developed the uncertainty principle, which states that it is impossible to precisely measure both the position and velocity of a particle at the same time.

- Alan Turing was an English mathematician who made major contributions to computer science and artificial intelligence. He developed the Turing machine, which is considered one of the first models for a computer, and he also broke the German Enigma codes during World War II and allowed British Government to decode German communications. His work laid the foundation for modern computing.

- Did you know the smallpox vaccine was invented by Edward Jenner in 1796 and has saved millions of lives since? It is considered to be one of the greatest medical discoveries ever made, as it helped eradicate a deadly virus that devastated many cultures throughout history. Jenner observed that milkmaids who had previously contracted cowpox were immune to smallpox, and he used this knowledge to develop a vaccine.

- The Hubble Space Telescope was launched in 1990 and has been providing us with incredible images of the universe ever since! It has enabled astronomers to make many new discoveries about distant galaxies, stars, comets and more by gathering data from the depths of outer space which would otherwise be impossible to obtain. The telescope has helped us gain a better understanding of the universe and its vast mysteries.

- Did you know that Robert Watson-Watt invented Radar in 1935? This revolutionary technology allowed us to detect objects from far away by bouncing radio waves off of them. Radar was a key factor in helping the Allies win World War II and is still used today to help us detect and track objects in the sky.

- Did you know that Nikola Tesla invented the alternating current (AC) electrical system? This revolutionary technology replaced the inefficient direct current (DC) system and allowed electricity to be transmitted over long distances. Tesla's invention changed the way we generate and use electrical power, and without it many of our modern-day conveniences would not exist.

- Louis Pasteur was a French chemist who developed a revolutionary method for preserving food called pasteurization. This process involves heating food to kill bacteria and other microorganisms that can cause spoilage. Pasteurization has been used for over a century and is still an essential part of food production and preservation today.

- In 1953, James Watson and Francis Crick discovered the double helix structure of DNA - the genetic material that makes up all living things! Their work revolutionized our understanding of genetics and sparked a new era of biomedical research. Thanks to their discovery, we now have a much more sophisticated understanding of how genetic information is stored and passed down through generations.

- Did you know that William Harvey was the first person to describe the circulation of blood in 1628? He correctly understood that the heart pumps blood around the body, which is then returned to the heart for re-oxygenation. His discovery was revolutionary and helped launch a new field of medicine called physiology, which has since become the cornerstone of modern medicine.

- Did you know that the invention of Velcro was inspired by burrs? In 1948, Swiss engineer George de Mestral created a fabric fastener after noticing how the tiny hooks on burr plants clung to his clothing and socks. This ingenious idea is still used today in a variety of applications - from fashion to space exploration.

- Alexander Graham Bell invented the telephone in 1876! This revolutionary technology allowed people to communicate over long distances using transmitters and receivers. His invention revolutionized communication and paved the way for modern telecommunications as we know it today.

- In 1831, Michael Faraday discovered electromagnetic induction - the principle that electricity can be generated by passing a magnet through a coil. This discovery paved the way for the modern electric generator and the widespread use of electrical power.

- Hippocrates, who lived in ancient Greece around 460 BC, is widely credited as the founder of modern medicine. He wrote about many medical conditions, including diabetes and epilepsy, and is considered the father of evidence-based medicine.

- In 1877 Thomas Edison invented the phonograph - a device that could record sound onto wax cylinders. His invention revolutionized the music industry and allowed people to experience sound in ways never before imagined.

- Did you know that in 1898 Guglielmo Marconi successfully transmitted a signal over long distance using radio waves? His invention was revolutionary and marked the beginning of modern radio technology, which has since been used for communication, entertainment, and navigation.

- In 1942 Enrico Fermi conducted the first nuclear chain reaction, paving the way for nuclear power and weapons. His work on fission helped unlock the potential of atom-splitting energy and ushered in a new era of scientific exploration.

- Edwin Hubble is credited with discovering that galaxies outside our own Milky Way exist. This discovery changed our understanding of the universe and revolutionized our idea of how vast and complex it is.

- In 1789 Antoine Lavoisier proposed the modern version of the law of conservation of mass, which states that matter can neither be created nor destroyed. His work helped revolutionize chemistry and has since been applied to many scientific disciplines.

- In 1938, German scientists Otto Hahn and Fritz Strassmann discovered the process of nuclear fission, the splitting of atoms. This discovery led to the development of atomic bombs and eventually ushered in a new era of nuclear weapons research and technology.

- In 1822, French mathematician Joseph Fourier developed the theory of heat conduction, which states that heat flows from hotter to colder objects. This discovery revolutionized the field of thermodynamics and has since been applied to many engineering fields, such as air conditioning and refrigeration.

- In 1839, Scottish physician James Simpson discovered chloroform - a colorless, sweet-smelling liquid used as an anaesthetic. His discovery revolutionized surgery and allowed medical procedures to be performed without causing pain.

- In 1896, French physicist Henri Becquerel discovered radioactivity - the spontaneous emission of particles from certain naturally-occurring elements. This groundbreaking discovery opened the door to new research in nuclear physics and ushered in a new age of atomic energy.

- In 1796, English physician Edward Jenner developed the world's first vaccine - a method of preventing infectious diseases by inoculating people with a weakened form of the disease-causing microorganism. This discovery revolutionized public health and has since saved millions of lives.

- In 1868, Russian chemist Dmitri Mendeleev developed the periodic table - a standard way of organizing the elements and understanding their properties. His work revolutionized the field of chemistry, making it easier for scientists to understand how matter behaves at a molecular level.

- In 1895, German physicist Wilhelm Röntgen discovered X-rays - high-energy electromagnetic radiation capable of penetrating solid objects to reveal images of bones and organs within the body. His invention revolutionized medical diagnosis, making it easier to detect diseases early on.

- In 1909, French physicist Jean Perrin proposed a theory of Brownian motion - the random movement of particles suspended in a liquid or gas caused by collisions with molecules from the surrounding medium. This discovery helped scientists understand the behavior of matter at a very small scale and shed light on many scientific phenomena.

- In 1903, American aviator and inventor Orville Wright and his brother Wilbur Wright achieved the world's first powered flight in an airplane. Their invention revolutionized transportation and changed the way people move around the globe.

- In 1917, Albert Einstein proposed his general theory of relativity, which states that gravity is caused by the curvature of spacetime. This revolutionary discovery has since been applied to many sciences and changed our understanding of the universe.

- In 1958, Jack Kilby invented the integrated circuit - a device that powers computers, phones, TVs and other electronic devices today. His invention ushered in a new era of computing and changed the way we interact with technology.

WORLD RECORDS

- The city of Tromso, in Norway, is known as 'the Paris of the North'. It is located above the Arctic Circle and experiences weeks with no night during summer, becoming a popular destination for tourists looking to witness the amazing phenomenon of the Midnight Sun.

- Mount Everest is the tallest mountain on Earth, with an official height of 8,848 meters above sea level. It is also the deepest mountain on land, as its peak extends almost 6.5 miles below sea level when measured from the center of the Earth.

- The Bald Eagle is the official national bird of the United States, symbolizing strength and freedom since 1782. It is not actually bald, but has white feathers around its head, which give it an appearance of baldness.

- The world's largest colony of penguins is located on Zavodovski Island, situated in the South Sandwich Islands in Antarctica. There are an estimated 7.5 million pairs of King Penguins living there, making it the most densely populated island on Earth for these animals.

- The Dead Sea is located between Israel and Jordan and is one of the world's most unique bodies of water. It contains 10 times more salt than any other sea on Earth and has such high concentrations of minerals that it is impossible to sink in, allowing anyone to float on the surface with ease.

- One of the most expensive paintings ever sold was Paul Cézanne's "The Card Players" which was bought by the Royal Family of Qatar in 2011 for a staggering $250 million dollars. The painting is considered to be an example of Post-Impressionism and is estimated to have been created between 1890 and 1892.

- The Ghent Altarpiece, otherwise known as "Adoration of the Mystic Lamb" was painted between 1426-1432 by Hubert and Jan van Eyck. It is a 15th century masterpiece that is often considered to be the first large-scale oil painting ever created, setting an important milestone in art history.

- Michelangelo's Sistine Chapel ceiling is one of the most iconic achievements in art. The masterpiece consists of more than 300 figures painted on a 12,000-square-foot ceiling and took the artist four years to complete.

- One of the most famous sculptures in history is Rodin's "The Thinker", which was first created in 1880 as part of his series called "The Gates of Hell". It has since become one of world's most recognizable works and is often seen as a symbol for thought and contemplation.

- Käthe Kollwitz was an influential German Expressionist who rose to fame through her paintings, woodcuts and drawings that focused heavily on social justice issues like poverty, war and death. Kollwitz is the only female artist to have a solo exhibition at the National Gallery in Berlin during her lifetime.

MONUMENTS

- The Great Wall of China is one of the most iconic architectural wonders in history. It stretches for more than 13,000 miles across 5 provinces in northern China, making it one of the longest man-made structures ever created.

- The Taj Mahal was built as a mausoleum by Mughal emperor Shah Jahan between 1632 and 1654 to commemorate his third wife Mumtaz Mahal. Over 7-8 million people visit the monument every year, making it India's top tourist attraction that year.

- The Leaning Tower of Pisa is one of the most recognizable monuments in the world. The structure began to lean due to a shallow, unstable foundation which caused it to tilt at an angle of over 5 degrees. The leaning began to increase during the 14th century but it was eventually stabilized in 2001.

- The Colosseum in Rome is one of the most iconic monuments from ancient times and still stands as a testament to Roman engineering. It was built between 70-72 AD and could hold up to 50,000 spectators at any given time, making it an impressive feat for its era.

- The Sagrada Família in Barcelona is an unfinished masterpiece designed by renowned Catalan architect Antoni Gaudí. Construction on the basilica began in 1882 and is estimated to be completed some time in 2026 after over 140 years of work.

- The Eiffel Tower is one of Paris' most famous landmarks and one of the world's most visited monuments. The tower was completed in 1889 and stands at a staggering 1,063 feet tall, making it the tallest structure in Paris.

- Stonehenge is an iconic prehistoric monument located in England that has fascinated people for centuries. It is estimated to have been constructed between 3000-2000 BC and consists of approximately 100 stones arranged in a circular form.

- Angkor Wat is a Hindu temple complex located in Cambodia which dates back to 12th century AD. It is renowned as one of the largest religious monuments ever created and covers an area of 400 acres, making it even larger than the Vatican City.

- The Great Pyramid of Giza is the oldest and only remaining monument from the Seven Wonders of the Ancient World. The pyramid was built around 2560 BC by pharaoh Khufu and stands at a staggering 455 feet tall, making it one of the largest structures ever erected.

- Chichén Itzá is an ancient Mayan city in Mexico that has been designated as a UNESCO World Heritage Site since 1985 It features numerous impressive monuments including El Castillo, a 75-feet step pyramid that is often considered to be one of the new seven wonders of the world.

- The Vatican City is an independent city-state located in Rome and home to the Roman Catholic Church's headquarters. It is one of the world's smallest countries, covering just over 109 acres, and houses some of the most important religious monuments in Christendom including St Peter's Basilica and Sistine Chapel.

- Machu Picchu is a 15th century Inca citadel located high in the Peruvian Andes which was declared a UNESCO World Heritage Site in 1983. This archaeological site has become one of South America's premier tourist attractions due to its impressive architecture and breathtaking views.

- The Panama Canal was opened in 1914 as a way to reduce sailing time between the Atlantic and Pacific oceans. It stretches 48 miles across the Isthmus of Panama and is considered one of the greatest engineering feats in history.

- The Empire State Building in New York City is perhaps the most iconic skyscraper in the world, standing at 1,454 feet and 102 stories tall. It was the tallest building in the world when it opened in 1931 and remained so for over 40 years, until the completion of the World Trade Center in 1973.

INTERESTING CURIOSITIES

- Did you know the world's oldest message in a bottle was discovered after 108 years at sea? Found off the shore of Germany by beachcombers, this 107-year-old message is believed to be from a German ship called Paula. It reportedly contained postcards and a call for help.

- The Titanic sunk on April 15th, 1912 but it wasn't until 1985 when an expedition found its wreckage over 12,500 feet below the Atlantic ocean's surface. After many years under water, many artifacts were recovered that can now be seen on display around the world.

- King Tutankhamun is one of Egypt's most famous leaders who lived 3,300 years ago. His tomb was discovered in 1922 by British explorer Howard Carter and it contained over five thousand treasures. This includes a mask with more gold than any other artifact from the period.

- Did you know that the world's first computer programmer was a woman named Ada Lovelace? She is believed to have written the very first algorithm for a computing machine in 1843, paving the way for generations of coders to come.

- The Suez Canal is located in Egypt and connects two major bodies of water: the Mediterranean Sea and Red Sea. It is one of the largest shipping canals in the world, but its construction took just 10 years to complete between 1859-1869!

- Did you know that the Berlin Wall divided East and West Germany for 28 years until it was finally demolished in 1989? The wall was 155 kilometers long and over 4 meters tall, separating families and friends who could not cross to the other side.

- Did you know that Genghis Khan is believed to be one of the most successful military commanders ever? Not only did he unite Mongolia under a single banner but his empire stretched from China to Europe!

- Apollo 11 was the first space mission manned by humans, landing on the moon in July 1969. This historic journey made Neil Armstrong and Edwin "Buzz" Aldrin the first men in history to set foot on Earth's natural satellite – an incredible accomplishment!

- The Eiffel Tower is one of the most iconic monuments in Paris, but did you know it was only meant to be a temporary structure? Built in 1889 for the World's Fair, it was never intended to be permanent and was almost torn down in 1909!

- Did you know that Antarctica is the coldest, windiest and driest continent on Earth? With temperatures dropping below -90 degrees Celsius in some regions, it's also one of the most inhospitable places on our planet. Despite this, there is an abundance of wildlife that call it home.

- Did you know that Napoleon Bonaparte was a French emperor who lived over 200 years ago? Across his reign he conquered much of Europe until his defeat at Waterloo in 1815. He was known for his military genius and strategy but also for his ambition and power-hungry nature – a fascinating historical figure nonetheless.

- Did you know that Mount Everest is the tallest mountain on Earth, reaching an altitude of 8,848 meters above sea level? Despite its immense height, experienced mountaineers have managed to summit this peak since its first successful ascent in 1953!

- Did you know that Albert Einstein is widely regarded as one of the greatest minds ever? He developed the Theory of Relativity which revolutionized our understanding of space and time, but he also worked on projects ranging from quantum mechanics to cosmology during his life-long pursuit for knowledge. Despite not being formally educated beyond secondary school, he is one of the most famous scientists in history!

- Did you know that on Earth, gravity is the force that binds us to the ground and keeps us in orbit around the sun? The moon's gravitational pull also causes tides to rise and fall each day, making it an essential part of life on our planet. It truly is a fascinating phenomenon!

- Did you know that there are over 100 billion galaxies in the observable universe? In comparison, there are only 7 billion people on Earth – quite a staggering difference! This means every person is outnumbered by 14 million galaxies! What an amazing thought.

- Did you know that hummingbirds are some of nature's most amazing creatures? Not only can they flap their wings up to 80 times per second, but they are also capable of flying backwards! Furthermore, the smallest species of hummingbird weighs in at just 2.4 grams – less than a US penny!

- The Mona Lisa painting is the most visited artwork in the world, with up to 10 million visitors a year. It is also one of the most valuable artworks, valued at over $800 million dollars. Created by Leonardo da Vinci between 1503 and 1517, this masterpiece has been prized for its mysterious smile that changes depending on how you look at it.

- Marcel Duchamp is considered the father of conceptual art. In 1917, he created one of his most famous works, "Fountain", a porcelain urinal that was rejected by an art show but later went on to become a classic example of Dadaism and one of the most important pieces of twentieth-century art.

- Mark Rothko is known for his abstract expressionist paintings filled with blocks of bright colors. His 1958 painting "White Center" sold at auction in 2007 for $72 million — making it the highest price ever paid for a post-war artwork at that time.

- Vincent Van Gogh is one of the most famous and influential artists in history, a post-impressionist painter whose works are instantly recognizable. His iconic "Starry Night" painting was created in 1889 and remains one of his best known and loved paintings today.

- Jackson Pollock was an abstract expressionist painter who revolutionized art with his drip-painting technique of pouring paint onto a canvas laid out on the floor. He produced some of the most expensive post-war artwork ever sold when his 1947 work "No. 5" sold for over $140 million.

- Pablo Picasso was a master of many styles, from cubism and surrealism to expressionism and modern art. He created one of his most famous works, "Les Demoiselles d'Avignon" in 1907 and it has been hailed as the first cubist painting ever made.

- Edvard Munch's iconic painting "The Scream" is one of the world's most recognizable pieces of artwork, depicting a figure with an agonized expression against a vibrant red sky. The original 1893 version of this painting sold at auction for over $120 million in 2012 — making it the most expensive piece of artwork ever sold at that time.

- Salvador Dali was a leading figure of the Surrealist movement and his works continue to inspire and influence artists today. One of his most famous pieces is "The Persistence of Memory" which depicts melting clocks against a dreamlike landscape. The 1931 painting is valued between USD 50M and USD 100M, becoming one of the most expensive Spanish paintings ever sold.

- Andy Warhol was a key figure in Pop Art whose larger-than-life personality made him one of the most recognizable figures in modern art. His 1962 work "Silver Car Crash (Double Disaster)" sold for over $105 million at auction in 2013, making it the second most expensive post-war artwork ever sold at that time.

- Claude Monet was a French Impressionist painter known for creating detailed paintings of nature. His iconic painting "Water Lilies" is one of his most recognizable works and it sold for almost $80 million in 2008 — making it the fourth most expensive Impressionist work ever sold.

- Frida Kahlo was a Mexican painter known for her self-portraits which enabled her to express her innermost thoughts as well as her physical and emotional pain. Her 1940 painting "Self-Portrait with Thorn Necklace" sold at auction in 2006 for over $5.6 million, becoming one of the highest prices paid for a Latin American artwork at that time.

- Rembrandt van Rijn was a Dutch Baroque painter renowned for his skillful use of light, shadow, and color. His 1658 painting "The Night Watch" is one of the most famous and recognizable works in Western art history and it currently owned by the city of Amsterdam.

- Michelangelo was a brilliant Italian Renaissance sculptor and painter who produced some of the world's most iconic works of art. From 1508 to 1512, he worked on his greatest project — painting the ceiling of the Sistine Chapel in Rome with some of the most spectacular frescoes ever created. This masterpiece continues to impress visitors from around the world today.

- Leonardo da Vinci was an Italian polymath whose genius spanned across many disciplines including painting, sculpture, architecture, engineering and mathematics. He is best known for his painting of the Mona Lisa and "The Last Supper", both of which continue to captivate viewers even today.

- Pablo Picasso was a Spanish cubist painter who famously said, "Everything you can imagine is real." His 1932 piece "Nude, Green Leaves and Bust" sold for almost $106 million in 2010, making it the most expensive artwork ever sold at that time.

MONEY AND CURRENCIES

- The idea of paper money was first proposed in China during the 11th century – a genius plan that allowed easier and faster transactions as opposed to using coins. It quickly spread throughout the world, becoming an integral part of modern life.

- Paper money was invented in China during Tang Dynasty (618-907) and it was called "flying money" or "jiao zi" – the first paper note had a value of one tael of pure silver. It wasn't until 1661 that European countries started issuing their own paper money.

- Ancient Rome used salt as currency – this is where the phrase "not worth his salt" originated from! Soldiers were paid with it, and it was considered so valuable, people would trade other commodities for it.

- The U.S. dollar is the world's most popular currency – accounting for nearly 85% of all transactions involving foreign exchange, making it a great choice in international trade and tourism.

- The smallest note ever printed was issued by the Bank of Canada in 1935, measuring just 2cm by 4cm - about the size of a credit card!

- In 2018, Bitcoin became the 6th most traded currency in the world – its popularity has grown immensely since its creation in 2009 as more people become invested in this digital form of cryptocurrency.

- In circulation since 1776, the British Pound Sterling is one of the oldest currencies on Earth – a symbol of Britain's heritage and its international presence.

- The world's first debit card was launched by Barclays in the UK in 1966 – it revolutionized the global banking sector, giving customers more control over their finances and transactions.

- The smallest denomination of a currency is the Iranian Rial, which is worth one-hundredth of an Iranian Toman – one Rial equates to about 0.00004 U.S Dollar!

- The most valuable currency in circulation today is currently the Kuwaiti Dinar – with 1 KD being equal to around 3 US Dollars, making it highly sought after by investors and tourists alike!

- In 1993, Zimbabwe introduced its own currency, the Zimbabwean dollar – which quickly became worthless due to hyperinflation and government mismanagement. It's still in circulation today, but worth far less than it was initially.

- Banknotes are made out of cotton and linen fibers because these materials are strong and durable enough to withstand wear-and-tear over time – even though many countries have switched to plastic notes for additional security benefits.

- In 1455, Johannes Gutenberg introduced metal movable type printing to Europe, revolutionizing the way books and paper money were created – allowing for mass production at a much faster rate than before.

- The first paper currency was introduced in Massachusetts in 1692 by the Province of Massachusetts Bay Colony - an innovative move that sparked a wave of similar initiatives across the entire United States.

- In some countries, it's illegal to deface or damage banknotes – destroying cash carries heavy penalties and could even result in jail time depending on the amount destroyed!

- The use of coins dates back over 2,500 years ago – some of the oldest coins ever produced are from ancient Greece around 600 BC and were made out of silver and gold.

- The U.S. Mint produces more coins than any other country, manufacturing over 20 billion every year – they're responsible for producing all of the nation's currency coins, including pennies, nickels, dimes and quarters!

- In 2009, the British Treasury issued a special "million pound note" in commemoration of the Bank of England's 300th anniversary – it featured a portrait of Sir John Houblon, the first Governor of the Bank of England.

- The largest coin ever made was produced by the Royal Canadian Mint in 2007 and is made from 99.999 percent pure gold - weighing one-hundred kgs and worth over $1 million!

- Ghana produces some of the most colorful banknotes on Earth – each with its own distinct design elements such as animals and cultural symbols.

- The euro is the second most traded currency in the world, after the US dollar – its usage has expanded rapidly since its inception in 1999 and is now used by more than 19 countries across Europe!

- The world's oldest surviving banknote dates back to 1661 and was issued by Stockholm Banco – it features the Swedish monarch of the time and is still in circulation today.

- The US dollar was officially adopted as the country's national currency in 1785 – it replaced the British pound, which had previously been used by the American colonies since 1690.

- Banknotes were originally made from animal skins, such as sheep or goat hides – this practice dates back to ancient China and is still used today for certain countries' currency notes.

- In 2013, the US Mint began producing a special $100 coin featuring Lady Liberty – it was the first time an African American woman was featured on an official US coin!

- The world's most expensive banknote is a rare 100 trillion Zimbabwean dollar note, issued by the central bank of Zimbabwe in 2008 – it's worth around $1 million dollars today!

- The fastest growing currency in history is Bitcoin, which was launched in 2009 – its value has surged over the last decade and is now one of the world's most valuable digital assets.

- Currency exchange rates are always changing due to fluctuations in global markets and geopolitical events – understanding how they work can help you save money when travelling abroad or engaging in international business transactions.

- The Euro is one of the newest forms of currency and was created in 1999. It is used in 19 of the 28 countries that are a part of the European Union.

- The Swiss Franc has been considered one of the world's most stable currencies for centuries and is used as a reserve currency by many governments around the world.

- Inflation is when prices rise over time which decreases purchasing power of a currency's value; deflation is when prices fall, which increases its purchasing power.

- Cryptocurrency, also known as digital or virtual currency, uses cryptography to secure transactions and prevent double spending of coins. Examples include Bitcoin and Ethereum.

- The world's first stock exchange was created in 1602 in Amsterdam, Netherlands when the Dutch East India Company opened a market where investors could buy and sell shares of their company.

- The London Stock Exchange is one of the oldest exchanges in the world, having been founded in 1801, and has become one of the largest stock markets by market capitalization.

- A gold standard is an economic system where a country's currency is backed by gold reserves and can be converted into the precious metal.

- The value of money is determined by its purchasing power, which can change due to factors such as changes in demand or supply, inflation, political events and technological advances.

- Inflation has been a part of most countries' economies for centuries, but some countries have managed to keep their currency free from inflation, e.g., Japan since the mid-1980s.

- Money laundering is when criminals try to hide the source or ownership of illegally acquired money through complex financial transactions that are difficult to trace back to the original

- The first use of paper money in the U.S was during the Revolutionary War when the Continental Congress issued a "Continental" currency which was not backed by gold or silver and subsequently lost its value due to hyper-inflation.

- The Federal Reserve System is the central bank of the United States and was established in 1913 to oversee the country's banking system, regulate banks, issue currency and set interest rates.

- The Bretton Woods Agreement of 1944 created a fixed exchange rate system for most countries allowing them to tie their currencies to the US dollar, which was tied to gold at a fixed price of $35/ounce; this system was abolished in 1971 when the US dollar became a floating currency.

- The International Monetary Fund was founded in 1945 with the aim of promoting international cooperation and maintaining financial stability; it provides loans, advice and technical assistance to its member countries to help them achieve economic growth.

- The Japanese Yen is the third-most traded currency in the world and has been a cornerstone of Japan's economy since its introduction in 1871; it was officially revalued after World War II to become a fiat currency not backed by gold or silver.

- The first credit card was introduced in 1950 by Diners Club and enabled customers to pay with a single card instead of carrying multiple pieces of tender when dining out; this system eventually spread to other businesses, leading to the development of the modern-day credit card system.

- A digital wallet is a mobile app used to store payment information such as debit/credit cards and provide users with a secure way to make purchases online or in stores using their phones. Examples include Apple Pay, Google Pay and Samsung Pay.

- Money laundering is the process of disguising illegally obtained money so it appears legitimate; it is illegal in most countries due to its potential use for terrorist financing or other criminal activities.

- Cryptocurrency is a digital form of currency, created and managed through the use of encryption techniques; unlike regular currencies, it is not regulated by any government or central bank and cannot be used to purchase goods or services directly. Examples include Bitcoin, Ethereum and Litecoin.

- Blockchain technology is the infrastructure behind cryptocurrencies; it is a secure database of records that are encrypted and linked together in "blocks" which can't be modified or deleted once added to the chain. It has been used to create decentralized applications such as smart contracts and non-fungible tokens (NFTs).

- A central bank digital currency (CBDC) is an electronic version of a national currency issued by a central bank that can be used for payments, transfers and investments; it could potentially reduce costs and simplify the way money is managed. Examples include the Bahamas' Sand Dollar, China's Digital Yuan and the European Central Bank's digital euro.

- Digital banking is an umbrella term for all financial activities conducted using digital technologies such as smartphones or computers; this form of banking has grown rapidly in recent years due to its convenience and accessibility. Examples include online banking, mobile banking and contactless payments.

- Money transfers are the movement of money from one account to another either electronically or through physical means; they can be used for international payments, remittances and other financial transactions. Examples include wire transfers, checks and bank drafts.

- Loan financing is a type of funding that involves borrowing money from another person or institution in exchange for repayment with interest; it can be used to finance large purchases such as cars or homes, pay off debt or start a business venture.

- Investment management is the process of managing investments by researching, selecting and monitoring different types of investments such as stocks, bonds and mutual funds; it is typically done with the help of a financial advisor.

- Financial literacy is an important part of being able to understand how money works and make informed decisions about managing finances; it involves topics such as budgeting, saving, investments and debt management.

- The global economy is the interconnected web of economic activities that take place between countries across the world; it's driven by various factors such as trade, investment and innovation. It has a major impact on all our lives as individuals, businesses and nations.

WONDERS OF THE WORLD

- Easter Island located off the coast of Chile has an enormous amount of Moai statues that have captivated visitors since they were first discovered in 1722 by Dutch explorers. It is believed that the statues were created by the Rapa Nui people to represent their ancestors and spiritual leaders.

- Angkor Wat is a temple complex located in Siem Reap, Cambodia that dates back to the 12th century and is believed to be the largest religious monument in the world. Its intricate architecture is a testament to the skill of its creators, the Khmer people.

- Chichen Itza located on Mexico's Yucatán Peninsula was once an ancient Mayan city that reached its peak between 600-1200 C.E. This city holds many mysteries such as their calendar system and knowledge of astronomy which can still be seen in the architecture of its temples and pyramids.

- The Acropolis in Athens, Greece is one of the most iconic structures from antiquity, topped by the Parthenon temple which was built to honor the goddess Athena between 447-432 B.C.E. Its ruins still stand today as a reminder of Greece's rich and varied history.

- The Statue of Liberty located in New York City is an iconic symbol of freedom around the world, given to America by France in 1886 as a sign of friendship between both countries. It stands over 300 feet tall and has inspired many for generations.

- Petra is an ancient city carved out of sandstone in Jordan that dates back to 6th century B.C.E and was the capital of the Nabataean kingdom. Its tombs, temples, and monuments are a testament to its past glory that continues to amaze visitors with their unique beauty.

- The Great Pyramid of Giza is the oldest and largest of the three pyramids located in Egypt and is believed to have been constructed between 2589-2566 B.C.E as a tomb for Pharaoh Khufu. It stands as one of the world's most amazing architectural feats even today.

- Uluru or Ayers Rock in Australia stands out as one of the most recognizable landmarks due to its immense size and red coloration created from iron oxide deposits in the sandstone. It is a sacred site to the Aboriginal people and they ask visitors to respect its cultural significance.

- Mount Fuji is an iconic mountain located on the island of Honshu, Japan that stands 12,388 feet tall and is an active volcano. It is a sacred site in Japan and has been the subject of numerous works of art, poetry, and literature throughout centuries as an embodiment of beauty and power.

- Christ the Redeemer statue is located in Rio de Janiero, Brazil and stands 98 feet tall atop Corcovado mountain overlooking the city below. It was completed in 1931 to honor Jesus Christ, symbolizing peace and brotherhood across Brazil and beyond.

- The Forbidden City located in Beijing, China was once the imperial palace during the Ming dynasty from 1420 to 1911 and housed 24 Chinese Emperors over that time period. Its immense size, exquisite architecture, and opulence are still striking today and it is a World Heritage Site.

- Angkor Wat located in Cambodia is a vast temple complex dedicated to the Hindu god Vishnu that dates back to the 12th century C.E. Its beauty and scale are breathtaking and it continues to be one of Southeast Asia's most popular destinations today.

POP CULTURE

- Did you know that the original design of Mickey Mouse was inspired by a pet mouse owned by Disney animator Ub Iwerks? His beloved pet mouse, which Iwerks named Mousey, had a spherical head and oversized ears just like the iconic cartoon character.

- Pop culture fans might be surprised to learn that The Simpsons is actually the longest-running American sitcom in TV history. Since its debut in 1989, it has aired over 700 episodes and spawned multiple films, books, and video games.

- Who would have guessed that the Broadway adaptation of Chicago was actually based on a play from 1926? The musical first premiered on Broadway in 1975 and went on to become one of the most successful stage productions of all time.

- Fans of the Harry Potter series might not know that J.K. Rowling was actually a single mother living in poverty when she began writing the books. It took seven years for her to complete them, but they went on to become some of the best-selling books in history and established Rowling as one of the wealthiest authors alive today.

- Before he became an actor, Sylvester Stallone worked as a lion cage cleaner in a traveling circus!

- Most people don't know that the song "Happy Birthday To You" was originally written as a Christian hymn in the late 1800s! The original title was "Good Morning to All". It wasn't until 1924 when the Hill sisters who wrote it copyrighted it and transformed it into the beloved birthday tune we know today.

- Before they became famous musicians, both Elvis Presley and The Beatles were rejected by a record label in the 1950s. In 1955, Presley was turned away by Sun Records, while three years later, The Beatles were rejected by Decca Records.

- Pop culture fans may not know that before Batman became a beloved superhero, he actually appeared as a villain in two 1940s films! He was first played actor Lewis Wilson and then replaced with Robert Lowery in the sequel.

- Did you know that "Game of Thrones" author George R.R Martin wrote most of his novels on an old manual typewriter? He still uses it to this day and keeps it stored underneath his desk for inspiration when he writes new stories.

- Most people are unaware that the famous film "Jaws" was based on a novel of the same name written by Peter Benchley. The novel was first published in 1974 and went on to become one of the best-selling books of all time.

- Few people are aware that singer Michael Jackson had planned to write an autobiography before his untimely death in 2009. He had already started writing it, but unfortunately never completed it due to his tragic passing at just 50 years old.

- Believe it or not, Marvel Comics creator Stan Lee actually came up with some of his most iconic superhero characters while he was serving in World War II! His creation Captain America was inspired by his service as an Army soldier during the war.
- Did you know that the classic video game "Pac-Man" was actually based on a real-life pizza? Its developer, Toru Iwatani, was inspired by the shape of a pizza with one slice missing to create the iconic character and his rounded maze.

- Before he became an actor, Arnold Schwarzenegger spent five years competing as a bodybuilder during the 1960s! He won several competitions including Mr. Universe in both 1970 and 1971 before beginning his acting career in Hollywood.

- Before she became an award-winning singer, Adele was a drama student at the BRIT School for Performing Arts and Technology in London. She later dropped out of school to pursue music full-time and hasn't looked back since.

- Did you know that the popular board game Monopoly was actually based on a real estate development project initiated by Elizabeth Magie in 1904? Her version of the game was designed to show players how monopolies can lead to financial inequality and economic disparity. It was called "The Landlord Game'

- Most people don't realize that the classic Disney song "Let It Go" from Frozen was actually written by husband-and-wife team Robert Lopez and Kristen Anderson-Lopez! They took home an Oscar for the song in 2014 and their work has since become beloved by millions around the world.

- Before he became a legendary actor, Steve Buscemi was actually a firefighter! He served with New York City's Engine Company 55 from 1980 to 1984 before leaving to pursue his dream of becoming an actor. He still volunteers at firehouses around America whenever possible.

- Godzilla is one of the most well-known films worldwide; what many do not know however is that it went through several name changes before reaching its final title! Initially called Gigantis–The Fire Monster, it changed to Godzilla: King of the Monsters before being shortened to simply 'Godzilla'.

- Michael Jackson is one of the best-selling music artists in history; his 1982 album Thriller sold 65 million copies worldwide and is certified 33x platinum in the United States alone!

- The first rap record released was 'Rapper's Delight' by The Sugarhill Gang back in 1979; it became a hit and revolutionised hip hop culture forever, paving the way for many others to follow suit.

- The 'Friends' theme song was written by Rembrandts who, at the time of recording, were completely unknown! They wrote it in one day and it went on to become a classic that has been covered countless times over the years.
- The 1998 film 'Shakespeare in Love' won seven Academy Awards; this included Best Picture, Best Actress (Gwyneth Paltrow), Best Supporting Actress (Judi Dench) and a nomination for Best Original Screenplay.

- Before becoming a global superstar, Jennifer Lopez was an unknown dancer; she made her debut as a fly girl on 'In Living Color' before launching her career as both an actor and singer, ultimately becoming one of the world's most successful entertainers.

- Elvis Presley was one of the first musicians to appear on television and he is credited with popularising rock 'n' roll; his early TV performances made him a household name, leading to his status as an international superstar.

- The 2009 sci-fi action film Avatar famously used pioneering technology that allowed actors to perform in a virtual world; this helped create its dazzling special effects which have since become iconic and revolutionary for the film industry.

- The iconic rock band Queen were originally called Smile and had a different lead singer before Freddie Mercury joined; they changed their name to Queen in 1973, shortly after the addition of Mercury on vocals, and the rest is history.

- The popular MTV show 'The Osbournes' was initially pitched as a scripted sitcom but producers realised that the real-life antics of Ozzy Osbourne and his family would be much funnier than any script could provide them with!

- Disney's classic movie 'Cinderella' was released in 1950; it became an instant success, garnering three Academy Award nominations for its music and becoming one of the most beloved Disney films of all time.

- The first movie to ever win an Academy Award for Best Picture was the 1927 silent movie 'Wings'; it was also the only silent movie to receive this award and is considered to be one of the greatest films of its era.

- The beloved children's show 'Sesame Street' premiered in 1969; it quickly earned critical acclaim for its educational content and has gone on to become a legendary, timeless series which remains popular across generations today!

- The Beatles famously performed their last live concert at Candlestick Park in San Francisco on August 29, 1966; they never returned to that stage or any other as a group before disbanding four years later.

- The groundbreaking sitcom 'I Love Lucy' was the first ever show to feature a pregnant woman on television; Lucille Ball's character in the show was famously expecting her second child and the show received a lot of criticism for its daring decision to include this plotline.

- Michael Jordan is famously one of the greatest basketball players of all time, but he initially retired from professional basketball in 1993 after winning three consecutive championships; however, he returned two years later and went on to win three more titles with the Chicago Bulls.

FUTURE AND TECHNOLOGY

- By 2035, the majority of humans will be able to access and control their own genetic code through personalized gene editing technology. This would allow them to customize their physical characteristics, health, and even intelligence.

- Scientists have recently created a 3D printer that can print organs using human cells with the aim of eventually being able to replace damaged or diseased organs with healthy ones.

- In 2021 many cars are beginning to feature driverless technology, but by 2035 completely autonomous self-driving cars could become the norm for most people's commute times.

- By 2030 scientists expect artificial intelligence (AI) to expand significantly beyond its current capabilities and start replacing more complex tasks usually done by humans.

- In 2020, a new technology called quantum computing was released and it is expected to revolutionize the world of computing – allowing computers to solve problems in minutes that would take a regular computer years to complete.

- By 2037 scientists expect robots to become adept at learning and performing complex tasks, making them an invaluable asset for home and commercial use alike.

- With the emergence of blockchain technology, many experts believe that by 2040 physical money may become obsolete with digital currency becoming the preferred method of payment for most people globally.

- By 2045 advances in nanotechnology will enable scientists to create tiny machines that can be sent into the human body to detect diseases, pinpoint treatment areas more accurately, and even repair damaged organs or cells.

- In 2023, a new type of super-fast broadband technology is expected to be released which will allow people to access the internet up to 300 times faster than current speeds.

- By 2050 scientists are expecting that autonomous robots could become an everyday reality for most people – from self-driving cars to smart homes with robotic assistants able to complete a wide range of tasks from cleaning to shopping errands.

- By 2035, experts expect computer software and hardware will become so advanced that it could enable online shoppers to create fully customizable products tailored specifically to their needs with 3D printers in the comfort of their own home.

- With advances in virtual and augmented reality, by 2040 many people will be able to experience virtual worlds, allowing them to take part in activities without ever leaving their home.

- In 2021 scientists have started researching bioprinting technology which could soon allow us to 3D print new organs and tissue structures such as skin or bone.

- By 2027 advances in artificial intelligence are expected to exceed human capabilities when it comes to making decisions and solving complex problems – drastically changing the way we work and live.

- In 2025 experts expect that most people's homes will feature smart technologies – from automated climate control systems with voice commands, personal assistant robots, and even robot vacuum cleaners.

- By 2030 autonomous drones may become a reality, allowing people to quickly and easily transport goods and products without having to wait for a truck or other form of transportation.

- By 2035, with the emergence of quantum computing, it will be possible for users to access incredibly powerful computers that can process data hundreds of times faster than current models – making tasks such as medical research much more efficient.

- In 2021 scientists have already begun to develop exoskeletons which allow people to increase their strength and endurance tenfold while also protecting them from potential injuries.

- By 2050 experts expect space exploration could become commonplace as advances in technology will make it possible for humans to explore far off planets and even inhabit outer space colonies.

- By 2040 experts expect that solar energy usage could reach its peak – with it becoming the most abundant renewable energy source globally.

- By 2025 self-driving cars will become a reality for many people, greatly improving safety and mobility for those who need it, as well as freeing up time spent commuting for other activities such as work or leisure.

- In order to address climate change, experts believe that by 2050 emissions from all motor vehicles will have to be reduced to zero in order for us to avoid an environmental disaster.

- By 2045 Scientists are expecting the development of advanced brain-computer interface technology which could allow users to control their computers and machines with just their thoughts – revolutionizing the way we interact with technology.

- By 2040 advances in renewable energy sources such as wind and solar power will become so efficient and ubiquitous that it could potentially end our dependency on fossil fuels, ushering in a new era of clean energy usage.

- In 2021 scientists have already begun developing nanobots which can enter the human bloodstream and detect disease markers more quickly than traditional methods, leading to earlier diagnosis and treatment of illnesses.

- By 2035 we could see the emergence of 3D printed food which would not only offer a more efficient way of producing food, but also reduce waste and make healthier meals available to more people around the world.

- In 2021 scientists have already begun researching ways to enable humans to directly control machines with their brainwaves – drastically changing the face of robotics and automation as we know it today.

- By 2050 experts predict that quantum computing will become commonplace in everyday life, allowing us to solve complex problems much faster than ever before – revolutionizing medicine, finance, transportation, energy and more.

- By 2040 experts predict that the use of blockchain technology will become widespread, allowing for secure transactions with high levels of transparency and security – drastically reducing fraud and other financial crimes.

- By 2030 genetic editing technology could become commonplace, allowing us to modify organisms' genes – revolutionizing medicine, agriculture, and potentially even human longevity.

- By 2045 advances in artificial intelligence will allow robots to autonomously carry out complex tasks without human supervision – changing the way we work and live forever.

- By 2035 experts believe that virtual reality will become mainstream and integrated with everyday life, allowing us to interact with the world in unprecedented ways.

- By 2050 advances in nanotechnology could enable humans to control matter on an atomic level – revolutionizing manufacturing processes and leading to entirely new products and materials never seen before.

- By 2040 advances in robotics will make it possible for machines to autonomously perform complex tasks such as surgical operations or construction work without human oversight – drastically increasing productivity while decreasing costs.

- By 2030 experts predict that advances in machine learning and artificial intelligence will enable computers to become smarter than humans – drastically changing the way we interact

ENTERTAINMENT & MOVIES

- The 'Friends' finale was the most watched TV episode the decade 2000s, with over 50 million viewers in the United States alone. It's been almost 20 years since it aired, but fans still talk about the show - and its lasting impact on pop culture - to this day.

- The Harry Potter franchise is the highest grossing film series of all time, earning more than $7.7 billion dollars at the worldwide box office. The franchise also has its own theme parks and several spin-off novels and films.

- The longest running Broadway show is "The Phantom of the Opera" which debuted in 1988 and is still running today, having been seen by over 130 million people in 35 countries.

- The Marvel Cinematic Universe is the highest-grossing movie franchise of all time, earning more than $28 billion dollars at the worldwide box office since 2008. The franchise includes 23 films and counting.

- The best-selling book of all time is the Bible, with over 5 billion copies sold. It has been translated into more than 724 languages and dialects, making it the most widely distributed book in history.

- The highest grossing animated film of all time is Disney's "Frozen", which earned over $1.2 billion dollars at the worldwide box office. It also ranks as the fifth-highest grossing movie of all time, behind four other major franchises from Disney and Universal Pictures.

- The highest grossing live-action movie of all time is "Avengers: Endgame", which earned over $2.8 billion dollars at the worldwide box office in 2019. It is also the fourth-highest grossing movie of all time, behind three other major franchises from Disney and Universal Pictures.

- The best-selling video game of all time is Tetris, with over 520 million copies sold across multiple platforms since its release in 1984. It has been ported to nearly every gaming system and mobile device in existence.

- The highest grossing concert tour of all time is U2's "Vertigo" tour, which grossed over $541 million dollars in 2005 and 2006. It was the band's most successful tour ever, breaking box office records around the world.

- The best-selling single of all time is Bing Crosby's "White Christmas", with over 100 million copies sold since its release in 1942. It has been recorded by numerous artists over the years, and remains one of the most beloved Christmas songs ever written.

- The most expensive film ever made is James Cameron's "Avatar", which cost over $350 million dollars to produce. It was a box office smash hit, becoming the highest grossing film of all time and earning more than $2 billion dollars at the worldwide box office.

- The best-selling toy of all time is LEGO, with over 600 billion pieces produced since its debut in 1949. The iconic building blocks have been beloved by children (and adults!) around the world for decades.

- The most popular theme park in the world is Disney World, with an estimated 58 million visitors each year. It includes four separate parks, two water parks, and over 25 themed resorts.

- The most visited museum in the world is the Louvre in Paris, with over 2.8 million visitors per year. It houses some of the world's most famous artwork and artifacts, including Leonardo da Vinci's "Mona Lisa" and the ancient Egyptian sculpture of Ramses II.

- The longest bridge in the world is the Danyang-Kunshan Grand Bridge in China, spanning over 164 kilometers (102 miles). It is part of the Beijing–Shanghai High-Speed Railway and opened to traffic in 2011.

- The fastest roller coaster in the world is Formula Rossa at Ferrari World in Abu Dhabi, with a top speed of 240 km/h (149 mph). It uses compressed air to launch riders from 0-100 km/h (62 mph) in just 2 seconds.

- The tallest building in the world is the Burj Khalifa, located in Dubai, United Arab Emirates. It stands 828 metres (2,717 ft) tall, and was completed in 2010 after 6 years of construction.

- One of the most-downloaded mobile game of all time is Angry Birds, with over 1 billion downloads across iOS and Android devices since its release in 2009. It has been ported to numerous gaming systems and spawned multiple sequels and spin-off titles.

- The most popular search engine on the internet is Google, with over 3.5 billion searches per day and over 2 trillion searches per year. It is the world's most used search engine, with an estimated 78% of global internet search traffic in 2019.

- The most popular animal in the world is the dog, with an estimated 900 million owned globally. They have been domesticated for thousands of years and are considered one of the most loyal animals on earth.

- The oldest known human-made object is a stone tool found in western Kenya, estimated to be 3.3 million years old. It is believed to have been used for cutting and skinning animals for food.

- The oldest known book in the world is the Diamond Sutra, a Buddhist text written on paper and dated back to 868 CE. It was printed using woodblock printing, one of the earliest form of printing in history.

- The most ancient cave art discovered is a red handprint in the Maltravieso Cave of Cáceres, Spain. It has been checked through uranium-thorium dating and found to be older than 64,000 years old - created by a Neanderthal.

- as of April 2021, the most-watched YouTube video of all time was "Despacito" by Luis Fonsi, featuring Daddy Yankee, with over 7.2 billion views. It's been surpassed by Baby Shark on January 13, 2022, which has surpassed 10 bullion views.

- The world's first feature film was released in 1912 and was titled "The Story of the Kelly Gang"; it ran for over an hour and a half, making it not only the first feature-length film, but also the longest non-interactive entertainment at that time.

- The first Academy Awards ceremony was held in 1929 and only lasted 15 minutes. It costed 5 dollars and 270 people attended! It was hosted by Douglas Fairbanks, who honored the film industry's most successful silent films.

- During the early stages of World War II, The Wizard of Oz was among the first Hollywood films to be shot in three-strip technicolor, a costly and intricate process that required a significant amount of time and resources. Despite the challenges involved, the resulting film sparked a revolution for its studio, MGM, and the film industry as a whole.

- In the movie Titanic, James Cameron was the artist who created the iconic sketch of Rose in the nude.

- In the movie Pulp Fiction, During the scene in which Uma Thurman's character is experiencing an overdose, it appears as though John Travolta injects her with a needle to revive her. However, in reality, Travolta was actually removing the needle from her arm, and the film was shown in reverse to create the illusion of the needle being inserted.

- While on set of the movie "The Godfather", director Francis Ford Coppola discovered a cat and gave it to Marlon Brando just before filming a scene. The cat became very fond of the actor and remained in his lap, purring so loudly that the crew was worried the noise would overpower the dialogue in the scene.

- David Fincher, the director of Fight Club, found the abundance of Starbucks locations in Los Angeles during the late 1990s to be excessive, so he included a humorous reference to the coffee chain in the film. Fincher claimed to have placed a Starbucks cup in every shot with the permission of the company, except for one scene in which a Starbucks shop was destroyed. In that instance, the fictional Gratifico Coffee was used instead.

- E.T. and Poltergeist have the same origin story. Steven Spielberg was initially going to produce John Sayles' script for Night Skies, a film about a family living in the countryside being invaded by aliens that could kill with a touch, but he ultimately decided to take a more family-friendly approach with the story and created E.T. The Extra Terrestrial. Sayles declined to rewrite the script, but Spielberg retained the concept for Poltergeist.

- The mask worn by Michael Myers in Halloween is actually based on William Shatner's face, specifically his portrayal of Captain Kirk in Star Trek. Due to the limited budget of the 1978 horror film, the art director purchased both a clown mask and a Captain Kirk mask and modified them to create the final version worn by Myers. The crew sprayed the mask white, adjusted the eyes and hair, and used it in the film to create a frightening appearance.

- Originally, Woody from Toy Story was intended to be a ventriloquist dummy. In early versions of the script, he was written as a sarcastic bully who tried to convince the other toys to turn against Buzz. However, the studio ultimately decided to change Woody into a more likable character.

- O.J. Simpson was a contender for the lead role in The Terminator, but director James Cameron ultimately decided against casting him because he didn't believe Simpson, who he described as a "goofy, kind of innocent guy," would be convincing as a cyborg assassin.

- R2-D2 and C-3PO from Star Wars can be spotted in Indiana Jones. If you look closely at the background in Raiders of the Lost Ark, you'll notice hieroglyphics featuring the likenesses of the robots in two scenes.

- The fire scene in Gone With the Wind was created by filming the burning of old sets that the filmmakers needed to clear out to make room for new sets. They filmed the destruction of these sets and used the footage to depict the burning of "Atlanta" in the film. It was a fortunate coincidence that this approach worked, as the filmmakers had already shot the scene before the cast for the movie was finalized.

- In The Wizard of Oz, Toto, the dog, was paid more than the Munchkin actors. The Munchkin actors earned $50 a week, which was a good wage for the time period, while Toto received $125 a week.

- The set for the 1923 silent film The Ten Commandments, including 21 replicas of the Sphinx, was buried underground for decades. The director, Cecil B. DeMille, believed the set was too valuable to be used by other filmmakers, and he decided it would be more cost-effective to bury the set rather than move it. The artifacts remained underground near the California coast for 94 years until they were discovered by archaeologists in 2017.

- Psycho was the first film to show a toilet flushing on screen. At the time, the Motion Picture Production Code prohibited the depiction of flushing toilets because it was considered to be inappropriate or dirty. However, Psycho played a significant role in challenging and eventually ending the censorship code.

- During a significant scene in Django Unchained, Leonardo DiCaprio's character becomes more animated as he smashes his hand on a table and cuts it on a glass. While this may appear to be special effects, it was actually an unplanned accident and DiCaprio really did cut his hand. The blood seen in the scene is real.

- During the production of the 1931 film Dracula, it was common for foreign language films to utilize the same sets and scripts as their English-language counterparts, but shoot their own versions at night rather than dubbing over the original footage later. As a result, Dracula was filmed in English during the day and in Spanish at night. The Spanish-language version of the film, which used the same set and script as the English version, was completed in about half the time and received much better reviews than the English version.

- The production of There Will Be Blood disrupted the filming of No Country for Old Men in Marfa, Texas in 2007. The two films, both considered instant classics and set in the western genre, were being shot in the same location at around the same time. A pyrotechnical test for There Will Be Blood produced a large smoke cloud that ended up in the shot for No Country for Old Men. As a result, the Coen brothers, the directors of No Country for Old Men, had to wait for the smoke to dissipate before continuing with their filming.

- Toy Story 2 almost suffered a major loss when a command entered into the "master machine" where the animation for the film was stored deleted 90% of the work done by the Pixar team. The team had a plan to restore the data from a regular backup, which would have resulted in only a half-day of work being lost, but the backup system had failed. Pixar did not have a copy of the Toy Story 2 files on its servers. Fortunately, the film's technical director had a copy of the work that she had been doing from home, and much of it was able to be restored.

- The population of clownfish in their natural habitats significantly decreased following the release of Finding Nemo, which features a clownfish as the main character. According to marine biologists, the number of clownfish on Australian reefs decreased by as much as 75% after the film was released.

- The script for the classic film Taxi Driver was written in just two weeks by screenwriter Paul Schrader. Schrader explained that he stayed with an ex-girlfriend and wrote continuously, completing the first draft in 60 pages. He then began the second draft immediately and finished it in less than two weeks.

- The Matrix's code originated from a sushi cookbook. The green digits that appear on the screen in the movie, which may seem like a mysterious code, were actually symbols from a sushi cookbook that were scanned by the film's production designer.

- In the past, the names of the Oscar winners were announced before the ceremony. In the early years of the Academy Awards, the organization shared the names with newspapers, but with the understanding that the newspapers would not reveal the names until 11 p.m. However, The Los Angeles Times broke this rule during the 1940 competition by announcing that Gone With the Wind had won before the award was presented, leading to a change in the rules that remains in place today.

- The movie Scream was originally going to be called Scary Movie. If the film had kept its original title, the Wayans brothers' parody of it would have needed a different name. The original movie's producer, Harvey Weinstein, who is now disgraced, was driving when he heard the Michael Jackson song "Scream" and decided he preferred that name for the film over its original title. The new title stuck.

- The bridge explosion scene in The Good, The Bad and The Ugly had to be filmed twice. The memorable moment in this Spaghetti Western, when Blondie and Tuco blow up the bridge leading to the cemetery where the gold is supposedly buried, had to be redone because the dynamite was detonated before the cameras were ready, causing the bridge to be rebuilt and the scene to be re-shot.

- Bill Murray was one of the actors considered for the role of Batman in the 1989 film. Along with Kevin Costner, Pierce Brosnan, and Mel Gibson, Murray was a candidate for the role of the superhero. However, when director Tim Burton joined the project, he chose Michael Keaton instead.

- Chewbacca in Star Wars was inspired by George Lucas' dog. Lucas had a large Alaskan Malamute that he would often take with him in the front seat of his car, which he described as being "bigger than a human being and very long-haired." Lucas' fondness for the dog inspired the relationship between Han Solo and Chewbacca in the films.

- Christian Bale used Tom Cruise as inspiration for his role in American Psycho. Bale stated that he was influenced by an interview Cruise gave on David Letterman's show, where he noticed Cruise's "very intense friendliness with nothing behind the eyes." This helped Bale shape his portrayal of the character in the film.

- Several British rock musicians have cameo appearances in the Harry Potter movies. The film series features many British character actors, and it also includes appearances by members of the bands Pulp, Radiohead, and The Weird Sisters. Jarvis Cocker, Steve Mackey, Jonny Greenwood, and Phil Selway can all be seen in Harry Potter and the Goblet of Fire.

- The roles of Butch Cassidy and the Sundance Kid were originally reversed in the script for the film of the same name. William Goldman's original script for the movie was titled The Sundance Kid and Butch Cassidy, but when Paul Newman, who was a very popular actor at the time, took on the role of Butch, the names of the characters were switched.

- Paranormal Activity is the most profitable film of all time due to its low budget and strong box office performance. The 2007 horror film had a return on investment of 19,758%, far surpassing the next most profitable film, The Gallows, which had an ROI of 6,843%. Paranormal Activity was made for just $60,000 and an additional $400,000 was spent on marketing, but it eventually earned over $89 million in revenue.

- Gene Hackman was initially slated to play Hannibal Lecter in The Silence of the Lambs. Anthony Hopkins ultimately took on the role of the brilliant and insane serial killer and made it iconic, but originally Hackman was going to play the part. Hackman had purchased the rights to the film and intended to direct it, but he decided that the character was too dark for his tastes and backed out of the project.

- The movie Up features a total of 10,297 individual balloons. Each balloon was hand-drawn by the film's animators, and the effects artist Jon Reisch stated that "the entire canopy is filled with balloons. We didn't just simulate the outer shell."

The animators took the time to count each and every balloon that appears in the film.

- During its management training program, NASA uses the movie Armageddon to challenge new managers to identify as many errors as possible. Over 168 errors have been identified in the film through this exercise.

- In the movie The Matrix, Kung Fu choreographer Woo-Ping Yuen initially declined to work on the film and asked for an extremely high fee in the hope that it would deter the Wachowskis. When this didn't work, Yuen made a seemingly impossible demand: he would only agree to work on the film if he had complete control of the fight scenes and was allowed to train the actors for four months before filming. The Wachowskis agreed to these terms.

- In Elizabeth: The Golden Age, when Elizabeth visits St. Paul's Cathedral, construction is taking place. In reality, St. Paul's was undergoing repair work at the time. The director, Shekhar Kapur, decided to take advantage of the situation and used real stonemasons and construction workers, outfitted in period costumes and using authentic tools, to cut stone that was actually being installed in the cathedral. The scene was improvised based on the real-life circumstances.

- While filming a scene for Django Unchained, Leonardo DiCaprio's character Calvin Candie smashed his hand on a dinner table and accidentally crushed a small stemmed glass with his palm, causing him to bleed. DiCaprio remained in character and continued with the scene, and director Quentin Tarantino was so impressed that he used this take in the final cut of the film. When he called "cut," the room erupted in applause.

- For his role in Forrest Gump, Tom Hanks did not receive a salary but instead received a percentage of the film's profits. This arrangement ultimately earned him around $40 million.

- To find costumes for 20,000 extras in the movie Schindler's List, the costume designer placed advertisements seeking vintage clothes. The poor economic conditions in Poland at the time meant that many people were willing to sell clothing from the 1930s and '40s that they still had in their possession.

- To prepare for his role as The Joker in The Dark Knight, Heath Ledger isolated himself in a motel room for about six weeks. During this time, he focused on understanding the psychology of the character and worked to perfect The Joker's voice and sadistic laugh.

- In John Wick 2, Keanu Reeves performed approximately 95% of the fight scenes himself. To get ready for the role, he underwent three months of training in Judo, Brazilian Jiu-Jitsu, marksmanship, and driving.

- In The Lord of the Rings: The Fellowship of the Ring, the cast often had to travel to remote shoot locations by helicopter. Sean Bean, who played Boromir, was afraid of flying and would only fly when absolutely necessary. During the filming of the scenes where the Fellowship is crossing snowy mountains, Bean would spend two hours every morning climbing from the base of the mountain to the set at the top, already dressed as Boromir. The crew, who were being flown up to the set, could see him from the helicopters.

- In the movie Pretty Woman, the scene where Edward (played by Richard Gere) snaps the necklace case down on Vivian's (Julia Roberts) fingers was improvised by Gere and Roberts's reaction (laughter) was genuine. The filmmakers liked the moment so much that they decided to include it in the final film.

- While filming The Revenant, Leonardo DiCaprio, who is a vegetarian, decided to eat a raw piece of bison liver. He also had to learn how to shoot a musket, build a fire, speak two Native American languages (Pawnee and Arikara), and study with a doctor who specialized in ancient healing techniques. DiCaprio has said that this was the hardest performance of his career.

- In The Imitation Game, Benedict Cumberbatch admitted that he had a breakdown and couldn't stop crying during one of the final scenes of the film. He said that he had grown very attached to the character and was overwhelmed by the suffering the character had endured and the impact it had on him.

- Henry Cavill refused to take steroids or use digital touch-ups to enhance his physique for his role as Superman in Man of Steel. He wanted to push his body to its limits and develop a physique that was worthy of the character, and he felt that using steroids or trickery would be dishonest. As a result, he trained intensely to build muscle for the role and refused to have any enhancements made to his shirtless scenes.

- In Slumdog Millionaire, Director Danny Boyle placed the money to be paid to the three lead child actors in a trust that would be released to them upon their completion of grade school at 16 years old. The production company also arranged for an auto-rikshaw driver to take the kids to school every day until they reached the age of 16.

- In The Martian, Matt Damon's character Mark becomes emotional when he hears Commander Lewis' voice during a scene. The other actors had already finished filming their scenes and their pre-recorded voices were played to Damon from inside his spacesuit. As Damon imagined his character's isolation on Mars for two years, coupled with the fact that he was only hearing pre-recorded voices of his co-stars, he became tearful. Ridley Scott was so impressed with Damon's performance that he only needed to do one take of the scene, which was ultimately used in the film.

- The Titanic movie, with the exception of the present-day scenes and the opening and ending credits, takes place in 1912 and has a runtime of two hours and forty minutes, the same length of time it took for the real Titanic to sink. The scene in which the Titanic collides with the iceberg reportedly lasted 37 seconds in real life, and this is also the length of the collision scene in the movie.

- During the production of Saving Private Ryan, Tom Sizemore was struggling with drug addiction. Steven Spielberg gave him a strict ultimatum: he would be required to undergo daily drug testing on set, and if he failed even once, he would be fired from the role of Horvath and the part would be recast and re-shot with a different actor, even if it was near the end of production.

- During the production of Wonder Woman, Gal Gadot was pregnant and participated in re-shoots for the movie, including stunts. Since her baby bump was visible, the crew created a costume with a green screen around her belly which was later removed in post-production.

- While in costume on the set of Maleficent, Angelina Jolie admitted to scaring young children, with one child reportedly saying, "Mommy, please get the mean witch to stop talking to me." However, Jolie's daughter Vivienne Jolie-Pitt, who played young Aurora, was the only child who was not scared of her.

- Before filming The Theory of Everything, Eddie Redmayne met with Stephen Hawking just once. Redmayne recalls that during the three hours they spent together, Hawking only spoke a few sentences, so Redmayne felt unable to ask him personal questions. As a result, Redmayne found other ways to prepare for the role. He lost 15 pounds, trained for four months with a dancer to learn how to control his body, met with 40 people with ALS, kept track of the order in which Hawking's muscles declined, and practiced contorting his face in front of a mirror for hours. Additionally, Redmayne remained motionless and hunched over between takes, so much so that an osteopath told him he had changed the alignment of his spine. Redmayne admits that he is "a bit of a control freak" and that his preparation for the role may not have been healthy.

- On the first day of filming The Devil Wears Prada, Meryl Streep told Anne Hathaway that she thought she was perfect for the role and was glad they would be working together, but then added that it would be the last nice thing she would say to her. The film featured a large number of fashion designers' clothes and accessories, making it the most expensively-costumed film in history. Streep later donated her wardrobe from the film to a charity auction.

- In order to make the boxing scenes in Rocky IV look realistic, Sylvester Stallone instructed Dolph Lundgren to actually hit him. However, a punch to the chest left Stallone in intensive care for four days.

- In order to prepare for her role in Black Swan, Natalie Portman trained as a dancer for a year and paid for the training herself until the film found investors. According to director Darren Aronofsky, Portman's dedication and enthusiasm were instrumental in getting the film made.

- To portray an out of shape middle-aged man in Cast Away, Tom Hanks stopped exercising and gained weight. Production was then halted for a year so that Hanks could lose 50 pounds and grow out his hair to depict his character's time on a deserted island.

- To prepare for his role in Terminator, Arnold Schwarzenegger spent months working with guns. During the first two weeks of filming, he practiced stripping and reassembling weapons blindfolded until he could do it automatically, like a machine. He also spent hours at the shooting range and practiced handling different weapons without looking at them when reloading or cocking. In order to play the role, Schwarzenegger also had to become ambidextrous.

- Paul Bettany has not seen the film Iron Man and is unaware of the plot. He has described his role as J.A.R.V.I.S. as the easiest job he's ever had, as he only worked for two hours and was paid a large sum of money. He then went on vacation with his wife Jennifer Connelly.

THANK YOU!

Thank you for reading our book! We hope you enjoyed reading it as much as we enjoyed writing it.

We would love to hear your thoughts, feedback or suggestions!

Please consider leaving us a review on Amazon to help us grow and improve.

Scan the QR code below or visit our website.

www.witwriters.com/surprisingfacts

Wit Writers

Leave a review on Amazon

Scan the QR Code

Made in the USA
Monee, IL
10 November 2023

46194993R00050